Aubrey Menen

Cities in the Sand

Title Page: Ruins of the Temple of Bel at Palmyra (Syria).

Contents

Of Past and Future Ruins 9

The Semites 12

The Invention of the Alphabet 14

Conversation with My Uncle 22

Tyre and Sidon 25

Two Kings 30

Sailors 45

Settlements 51

The Tophets 56

The Punic Wars 64

Leptis Magna 67

The Basilica 89

The Harbour 102

Wild Beasts 109

Commodus 117

Didius Julianus   127

Septimus Emperor   137

Caracalla   150

Elagabalus   155

Alexander Severus   164

Taxes   169

Timgad   173

Soldiering   182

The Baths   191

The Triumph of the East   199

Palmyra   202

A View from Palmyra   226

The Empire Collapses   233

Odenathus   236

Zenobia   240

The Sands   251

Epilogue in Petra   255

A Short Reading List   260

List and sources of illustrations   261

Index   270

Chronology

BC c. 3500	Semitic migrations to Egypt and Tigro-Euphrates valley
BC c. 2500	Semitic migrations to Syria and Palestine
BC c. 2000	Earliest settlement at Palmyra of an urban nature
BC c. 1300	Approximate date of founding of Tyre
BC c. 974–c. 937	Reign of King Solomon
BC 814–813	Probable date of founding of Carthage
BC c. 500	Probable era of founding of Leptis Magna, but it may be earlier
BC c. 500	Earliest tombs at Petra
BC 264–241	First Punic War
BC 218–201	Second Punic War
BC 149–146	Third Punic War
AD 100	Founding of Timgad
AD 106	Petra conquered by Romans

The Roman Emperors from Marcus Aurelius to Aurelian

Marcus Aurelius	AD 161–180
Commodus	AD 180–193
Pertinax	AD 193
Didius Julianus	AD 193
Septimius Severus	AD 193–211
Caracalla	AD 211–217
Macrinus	AD 217–218
Elagabalus	AD 218–222
Alexander Severus	AD 222–235
Maximinus	AD 235–238
Balbinus	AD 238
Maximus	AD 238
Gordian III	AD 238–244
Philip the Arabian	AD 244–249
Decius	AD 249–251
Gallus	AD 251–253
Aèmilianus	AD 253
Valerian	AD 253–260
Gallienus	AD 253–268
Claudius Gothicus	AD 268–270
Aurelian	AD 270–275

Leptis Magna sacked by the Asturians, a tribe from the interior	AD 363–366
Vandals occupy Leptis Magna	AD 455
Leptis abandoned by its inhabitants	AD 523
Palmyra surrenders to Khalid ibn al-Walid, commander of Abu Bakr, the first Caliph	AD 634

Of Past and Future Ruins

In the 1940s, Rose Macaulay wrote a book about ruined cities and the pleasure to be found in them. Some she had seen herself: others she had not and for these she relied on writers who had, quoting from their books. It is an alluring volume. Navigating its pages, I found it almost impossible to resist the Scylla of Rose Macaulay's personal charm and the Charybdis of her beautiful prose. But, binding myself to the mast, I went through the book again, for it disturbed me.

I found there was something in common with everybody she quoted; something which I did not share at all. They felt superior to what they saw. Their own civilization, they thought, was so much better than the ones they saw in ruins. Besides, it would last longer. As they walked among the ruins in their veils and sun-helmets, mentally polishing their adjectives, one could almost hear them saying, 'There, but for the grace of my excellent education, my humanitarian views, and my holdings in gilt-edged, go I.'

Then came the bombing of London. One of the bombs fell on Rose Macaulay's house and destroyed it. It was not a ruin in which she could take any pleasure at all. But she was an honest writer and she felt bound to take a walk among the ruins of London and attempt to describe them, in order to round off the book. The task defeats her, and she escapes it by clothing the blackened masses with imaginary creatures and wildflowers. She ends her book abruptly. Ruins, she says, to be enjoyed, must be 'softened by art.' They must be a 'fantasy, veiled by the mind's dark imaginings.'

I have never felt that, and that is why the book had disturbed me. I have lived in two diverse civilizations, that of India, and the West. I have never felt that either was better, or more permanent, than those that have gone before. I have lived for many years in Rome. Forty feet down, below the table at which I am writing this page, are the remains of Roman houses. Every day in these years I have studied a ruin or read a book of history. I have never felt that the classical civilizations improved on ours, or that we have improved on theirs. The civilizations that mankind has set up are all a sorry catalogue of missed chances. The bomb on Rose Macaulay's house is the customary answer to all our hopes. It missed, by good fortune, the writer. The next bombs will not.

A few years ago, an English boy of fourteen came out to spend a holiday in Rome with me to continue his excellent education in the same way that Gibbon did, namely, to make the Grand Tour. I showed him Rome, and Naples and much else. Then one day he said that, for all the teaching he had received from his schoolmasters and me, he did not feel that he knew what it was all about. Would I show him?

After much thought, I boarded a plane and took him to the concentration camp at Dachau, in Germany. In the crematorium, I told him that, little as he could believe his eyes, this had actually happened. Moreover, though it might not happen again in my lifetime, there was every chance that this, or worse, could happen once more in his.

I confess that, once out of the place, my duty (as I conceived it) done, I felt I had been too pessimistic. There was, after all, America. Today, I have read my newspaper, and I find that at the very time that I stood with the boy in the crematorium, the President of the United States was sitting round a table in the White House, judiciously weighing the pro's and con's of unleashing nuclear warfare on the world in North Vietnam. We escaped that time, as Rome escaped sacking by Attila the Hun. On both occasions, it was a pretty near thing.

So in this book I do not intend to spend much time veiling anything with imaginations of my mind, dark or light. I shall take you on no expeditions by moonlight. We shall be in the broad day. I shall try to people the streets, the temples, the forums and the prisons with the persons who once lived there. I shall do my best to describe their lives, their loves, their hopes and their terrors. They will be found to be very like our own. Those people, too, like us, lived in a world which had once seemed safe and secure, but which was slowly, piece by piece, falling about their ears. They, too, did not know where they were going, but divined it was not likely to be very pleasant. They, too, longed for peace and quiet and a million dollars in the bank.

I shall therefore be practical, not romantic. I shall have to be, for the people with whom I shall mainly be dealing belong to the most practical (and perhaps the most astonishing) human groups in history – the Semites. They were so practical that without them I could not be writing these words, nor could you be reading them. Among the many remarkable things they did was to invent the alphabet.

The Semites

I am aware that 'Semite' has been used in the past as a dirty word, or at least, a grubby one. I have learned that to my cost. I have several times visited Jerusalem, usually when Arab and Jew were shooting at one another. I have talked to both. Early on in my visits I would make an attempt to cool the atmosphere by remarking that both Arabs and Jews were of one family, the Semites. I soon learned better. There, in Jerusalem, 'Semite' was not only a dirty word, it was a fighting word.

All the same, I intend to use it, for I am quite sure that as the monstrous prejudices of the twentieth century die away and we move into the twenty-first (if we ever are allowed to see it), then the word 'Semite' will have as glorious a connotation as we give today to the words 'Roman' and 'Greek'. More glorious, perhaps, because it is doubtful if the Romans and Greeks have really much to do with our way of life. The Semites made it.

Let us go back to Noah. He did not exist, but he is convenient. Noah begat three sons, Ham, Shem and Japhet. These three begot a vast progeny who did very well until, in Babel, they decided to build a tower. They were so near Heaven that Jehovah, fearing that His peace would be disturbed, stopped the building by striking them with a confusion of tongues.

The picture we have is of people vainly attempting to communicate, and not succeeding. But it is not quite true. The descendants of Shem (or more correctly, Sem, as the Vulgate has it) would have found that, after the disaster, although there were a number of tribal dialects, one tribe could, with an effort, make out what other descendants of Sem were saying.

The begetting went on. The descendants of Sem begat the Assyrians, the Babylonians, the Arameans, the Canaanites, Phoenicians, the Arabs, and the Hebrews. The Arabs begat Haroun-al-Rashid and the Prophet Mohammed. The Hebrews begat Jesus and Karl Marx. Now, if you will take a terrestrial globe and turn it slowly, you will see that the descendants of Sem have done the thinking for the greater part of the human race.

It is going to take the descendants of Ham and Japhet some time more to admit (and even some of the descendants of Sem) but there it is.

If we do not believe that the Semites came from Ararat, then we have to acknowledge that we are not at all sure where they did come from. At the dawn of history, we find Semitic languages being spoken along the edges of Arabia, along the eastern border of the Mediterranean, inland in what is now Syria and farther east to Mesopotamia. This is neat enough but, confusingly, some of the earliest evidence also comes from East Africa. So the Semitic-speaking peoples may have come, like the Arabs, from the desert of Arabia. This is more likely. In spite of T. E. Lawrence and other fine writers, the desert is a dreadful place in which to live, and people who are forced to do so are consumed (again like the Arabs) with a desire to get out of it and settle in more comfortable quarters. The desert, then, would account very well for the fact that these peoples migrated and spread. We cannot say. We know less about the early history of Arabia than of almost any country in the world.

It will be noticed that I have used the rather clumsy phrase, 'the Semitic-speaking peoples'. I shall drop it in preference for 'the Semites' but I must make clear what I mean by that, or, more importantly, what I do not mean.

The Semites are not a 'race'. They cannot be distinguished by having, say, a hooked nose. Some, indeed, have remarkably straight ones. That is something of a blessing, for the concept of 'race' has led to more stupidities in human history than any other factor. They are, instead, a people bound together by a basically common tongue, and a way of looking at the world, or, more precisely, looking beyond it. They are an intensely religious people. Religion may take many forms, from the Talmud, and the Koran, to the Sermon on the Mount and burning babies alive and putting their bones reverently in pots. But whatever they believed in, they believed intensely. Without religion, they would have had no backbone.

1 *A Semitic slave in Egypt* c. *1150 BC; faience tile from Thebes.*

The Invention of the Alphabet

I know that to many people nowadays this will seem a depressing trait. But we must beware of a trap that has been built into most of our minds by our upbringing. We tend, when thinking of the Semites, to dwell too much upon the Jews. The Jews, however, were far from typical Semites. They were much too unfortunate. The lands they conquered with enormous effort never did flow with milk and honey. The other Semites rolled in luxury. The Jews were always the poor relation. It would seem that they had a little money in the time of Solomon, but even then their riches were not spectacular. The Book of Kings makes a great parade of the building of the Temple. From the details given there, some dedicated men have built a large and accurate model of it as rebuilt by Herod. It can be seen on a hilltop outside Jerusalem. I have studied it. Although the Temple must have been costly to build, it could never have been dazzling in its splendour. This poverty of the Hebrews played a large part, I think, in making their religion puritanical and censorious. If one's neighbours flourished like the green bay tree, clearly they were wicked.

It must have been particularly galling to live so comparatively close to such places as Tyre and Sidon. These were inhabited by another Semitic people, the Canaanites, and luxury abounded. As became rich men, their religion was a comfortable and even lively affair. Some of their temples were brothels, both women and boys being among the prostitutes. This practice seems to have disturbed nobody in antiquity, except the Jews, who listed it as among the abominations indulged in by the dissolute capitalists. For that is what the Canaanites were.

2 The transport by river craft of cedarwood; alabaster relief from the palace of King Sargon II (721–705 BC), at Khorsabad (Iraq). ⟩

4 *Cedars in present-day Lebanon, where they have become extremely rare.*

They lived in a stretch of coast which we now call the Lebanon. It was fertile. It grew great forests of which the cedars of Lebanon have echoed down history. But it is not very big. It was limited by a range of mountains at its back, so that its width varies from 30 miles to a mere 7. It soon grew too small for its population. Had the Canaanites relied upon the produce of the land, they would have been not much richer than the Hebrews.

But they took to the sea, having some fine harbours. They were within easy reach of Egypt, where trees were scarce. They cut their cedars and shipped them to Egypt, carrying back in return some of the limitless wealth of that kingdom. Soon they expanded their trade to other places in the Eastern Mediterranean.

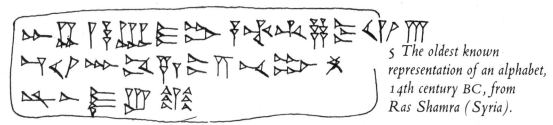

5 *The oldest known representation of an alphabet, 14th century BC, from Ras Shamra (Syria).*

Canaanite sailors regularly plied fixed trade-routes at certain seasons of the year, while back at home others financed the expeditions and, like the Merchant Adventurers of Elizabethan times, pocketed the proceeds. It was a tranquil life. The Book of Judges rather enviously remarks of another people, 'Quietly they lived, in the manner of the Sidonians, careless and secure and in the possession of riches.'

Perhaps it was this quiet life that gave them the time to work out one of the most important inventions in all history, the alphabet. The Egyptians with whom they traded had invented a system of writing which we know as hieroglyphics. It was remarkably beautiful, but very clumsy. Broadly speaking, it consisted of drawing a small, stylized picture of the thing to be described. It developed somewhat from this simple beginning but it could not develop very far. The drawing for an object began to be used to represent the initial sound of the word wherever it was used, but writing in hieroglyphics still took up an immense amount of time, even when the pictures were reduced to scribbles.

About the second millennium before Christ, the Canaanites hit upon an entirely new system, in which the sounds of the language were represented by letters, or, in the case of complex sounds, by a combination of the same. The symbols were of the utmost simplicity.

We cannot be quite certain that the Canaanites invented the alphabet out of thin air. An inscription has been found in Sinai which supports the theory that some rudiments of the idea were already present. But this is very uncertain and is still a subject of dispute among scholars. What is sure is that the Canaanites made the alphabet a workable thing, and put it to use.

The idea was so valuable it soon spread, aided by the trading visits of the Canaanite sailors. It was used in the Aegean islands, where it gave rise to the Greek alphabet and thus, passing on to the Romans, to our own ABC. It did not stop there.

18

Hebrew letter	Hebrew	Phonetic value	Ahiram	Elibaal (Osorkon bust)	Shipitbaal	Mesha	Kara Tepe bilingual	Punic	Neo-punic	Early Greek	Modern Greek	Modern Roman	Greek letter
aleph	א	ʾ	ΚΚ	∢	ΚΚ	∢	∢	∢	Ϗ	∀	A	A	alpha
beth	ב	b	99	9	9	9	9	9	9	Β	B	B	beta
gimel	ג	g	⌐	⌐	∧	⌐	⌐	⌐	∧	Γ	Γ	G	gamma
daleth	ד	d	◁	Δ	◁	Δ	◁	Δ	Δ	Δ	Δ	D	delta
he	ה	h	∃∃			∃	∃	∃	Я	∃	E	E	epsilon
waw	ו	w	ΥΥ	Υ	ΥΥ	Υ	Υ	Υ	У	F		V	digamma
zayin	ז	z	I		I	II	I	I	⌐	I	Z	Z	zeta
heth	ח	ḥ	⊟Ħ		⊟	Ħ	Ħ	Ħ	Я	日	H	H	eta
teth	ט	ṭ	⊕		⊖	⊗		⊙	⊗	⊗	Θ		theta
yodh	י	y	ι	ι	ι	ι	ι	∼	∼	ς	I	I	iota
kaph	כ	k	Ѱ	Ѱ	ѰѰ	У	У	У	У	Κ	Κ	K	kappa
lamedh	ל	l	L	L	L	6	C	ℓ	∧	∧	L	L	lambda
mem	מ	m	ϟϟ	ϟ	ϟϟ	ϟ	ϟ	ϟ	×	ℳ	M	M	mu
nun	נ	n	ϟ	ϟ	ϟ	ϟ	ϟ	ϟ	∫	ℳ	N	N	nu
samekh	ס	s	∓		∓		∓	∓	∓	Ξ			xi
ayin	ע	ʿ	Ο	Ο	Ο	Ο	Ο	Ο	∪	Ο	Ο	Ο	omicron
pe	פ	p	))	)	))	⌐	⌐	⌐	⌐	⌐	Π	P	pi
tsade	צ	ṣ				∽	∽	∼	⌐	Μ			
qoph	ק	q			φ	φ	φ	φ	φ	φ		Q	
resh	ר	r	9	9	99	4	9	9	9	Ρ	P	R	rho
shin	ש	š	W	W	WW	W	W	Ψ	ℎ	Ƹ	Σ	S	sigma
tau	ת	t	+X	×	+X	×	×	†	ℓ	T	T	T	tau
Probable dates of inscriptions			early 10th cent.	c.915	end of 10th cent.	c.830	8th cent. B.C.	5th cent. & later	2nd cent. & later	8th cent. B.C.			

6 *Table showing the development of the alphabet from its Semitic origins onward.*

7–10 *Various forms of the ancient alphabet: left, the inscription on this model of a cylindrical watchtower from Carthage (4th-3rd century BC) shows Punic alphabetical script; below, the 13th-century BC sarcophagus of King Ahiram of Byblos bears a Phoenician inscription along the side of its lid – its transcription is shown right; far right, this fragment of an inscribed slab (4th-3rd century BC) is regarded as an exceptionally good example of Punic lettering.*

Conversation with My Uncle

These remarkable people did not confine their trading to Egypt and the Aegean. They drove their fragile ships to Italy and Sardinia. They landed among the wild men of North Africa. They traded on the shores of Spain; ventured further, out into the Atlantic, and from there to the mists of Brittany and the North Sea. They turned south to Arabia and Persia. They pushed on down the Indian Ocean till they came to Malabar, that we now call Kerala. Everywhere they spread the alphabet.

These voyages were as epic as those of the Norsemen, yet they are nowhere celebrated. There are no poems about them. Nobody has used them for a film. Virtually nobody has written about them, for the facts are buried in a handful of books that are of the dustiest and driest form of historical writing. The reason is that the Canaanites killed nobody, burned down no cities, and stole no land. If they set up a settlement, they did not even buy the property. Carthage, which was one of the places they set up, paid rent to the original owners for centuries. Their only interest was in trade.

I have said that the Canaanites reached Kerala, deep in the south of India. Now that is where my family comes from. I was walking through our family lands one day with my uncle. I was twelve years old. My uncle was dressed in a single cloth of cotton that hung from his waist and fell to his ankles, the orthodox dress of the Nayars, to which caste we belonged. He was, as usual, talking about our family.

He pointed to a climbing plant, rather like a vine. He asked me if I knew what it was. When I said I did not, he broke off some pellets and gave them to me to eat. They burned my tongue.

'It is pepper,' he said. 'It's the finest pepper in the world. It always has been. We have been selling it for two thousand years.'

Now I had grown to be disbelieving about the immense antiquity of our family. True, we had been there in Kerala when Vasco da Gama had sailed in to Calicut: we plotted to kill him. But that, after all, was not so very long ago. Two thousand years was another matter. Small boys of twelve do not say much, but they can look very sceptical indeed. My uncle had no difficulty in reading my thoughts.

So he took me to one of the great, bare family houses. He squatted on a cement floor by an old wooden chest. From out of this, he took a small leather bag. He told me to hold out my hands and then he poured a heap of coins into them. They were silver, very worn, with a head stamped on them. I read the inscription and even with my schoolboy Latin I could see that they were coins of Augustus Caesar.

'They were found,' said my uncle, 'hidden away in an old temple, not a mile from here. The Romans had a passion for our spices. So we sold them to traders who sold them to the Romans. We still do, though the Romans are called Italians now. At least,' he said, and interrupted himself with a long, luxurious Kerala yawn, 'at least I *think* we do. Trade doesn't interest me. I leave all that sort of thing to the factor.'

The factor was a stocky Englishman in khaki shorts who spoke far less grammatical English than my uncle, and was very conscious of the fact. He was known as the *box-wallah*, the fellow with a little box in which he collected samples and invoices. He came once a year and he was treated with the barest civility, because he was in *trade*.

My uncle was a highly educated man. He could read and write Sanskrit, a most difficult tongue. I think he would have been upset to know that common traders had brought him its alphabet, because it was the Canaanites who had brought that Roman money to Kerala and exchanged it for our pepper.

And that is the trouble. We nowadays live in a commercial civilization. The great majority of us spend our lives buying and selling, or in making things to be bought and sold. But we are educated as though we were all cultured gentlemen like my uncle, strutting about our estates. We are taught some ancient history, but it is the sort that pleased generations of country gentlemen – the history of Caesars and Pharaohs, wars and empires, writers and artists. Each day when I leave my house here in Rome, I see earnest people dutifully looking at the Colosseum, the Forum, the Palatine or tramping around the museums of classical art. They are all thinking hard, or wishing they could. Yet there is one monument in Roman which should stir our imaginations above all others. It is a hill called Testaccio. It is 35 metres high and covered with grass and plants like any other hill of earth and stone. But if you climb its sides and kick the slopes with your foot, you will turn up the handle of an amphora, the earthenware jars in which the ancient traders brought wine and oil and a dozen other products to Rome. You may put one in your pocket without breaking any law – the whole huge hill is made up of broken pottery. Hard by, on the Tiber, was a port. For some reason that we do not know, potsherds were piled up here, till they made a hill.

It is so little visited that the municipal authorities considered it a good place to build its slaughterhouses. It is so neglected that the roads around it have become the most squalid sight in the city.

Tyre and Sidon

The two principal cities of the Canaanites in their early centuries were Tyre and Sidon. Practically nothing remains of them today, but a walk through their market-places when they flourished must have been full of fascination. A look at the map will show how conveniently they were placed between the eastern and the western worlds. The Canaanites were the go-between. The west, then, was barbarous. But there was silver in Spain, tin in England and iron in Sardinia and Elba. The inhabitants of these places had little idea of the value of these things, an admirable situation for a businessman. The Canaanites would beach their ships. The inhabitants would come down from the hills. They would lay their metals in piles and then retreat, back to their villages. The Canaanites next would land, inspect the offering and judge its value. They would bring out the cloth, the trinkets, the pots and other gee-gaws which the inhabitants wanted, and lay them, too, in piles. This done, they went back to their ships and waited. The inhabitants would steal back again, turn over the piles and decide if they were satisfactory. We may be sure that they took the Canaanites for fools, exchanging such desirable things for stones: and it follows, as night the day, that the Canaanites took them for a ride, as businessmen always do when the customer is sure he is dealing with a simpleton. The Canaanites would load their ships and sail back to Tyre and Sidon.

There they would meet a more romantic sight. There were the exquisite linens of Egypt of a fineness that has never been matched. There were elephant tusks from Africa, the skins of lions and panthers, fine wines from the Aegean, and painted Greek cups to drink it from. Above all, there were jewels from the Orient: pearls, diamonds, emeralds, the rubies of India, together with things

11 *Map showing the orbit of Phoenician trade and settlement.*

MACEDONIA

GREECE

ASIA MINOR

Ephesos

Aradus

Byblos
Sidon
Tyre

Palmyra

Jerusalem

Petra

Alexandria

R. Nile

EGYPT

Thebes

12–14 'Murex trunculus', the Phoenician shellfish which was used in producing the characteristic red dye. The jug from Citium (Cyprus) is painted with this dye (8th-7th century BC). The obverse of a shekel from Tyre, c. 460 BC, shows a dolphin leaping over the waves and below it a Murex trunculus.

15 This shekel from Tyre (reverse of Ill. 14), c. 460 BC, shows an Egyptian-type owl, crowned with a crescent, carrying a crook and flail.

just as precious, such as frankincense to perfume religious rites and to keep the smells of open sewers away from sensitive nostrils. And, of course, pepper.

But life in Tyre and Sidon was not all chaffering. There were artisans. From what little remains of their work, they never were very good ones. Like the rich in all ages, the Canaanites bought their luxury goods from abroad. But there was one industry that left its mark on the ancient world, and even on ours. There was a shellfish in the waters of Tyre and Sidon that produced a particularly intense and pleasing dye. It was very expensive and thus to wear clothes tinted with it became a measure of one's wealth, and, hence, one's status, so much so that in the Roman world it was reserved, by law, to the élite. Only they were allowed to wear it, usually as a deep band around the hems of their togas. Emperors, of course, could wear as much as they pleased, and even hang their walls with it. We still speak of 'being born in the purple.'

However, it was not purple. For centuries, historians have thought it was. But in modern times, archaeologists have been sufficiently curious to gather the shells, crush them, and extract the dye. It was red, a peculiarly intense red, very like the colour of the robes of Cardinals in full state. It still is a very flattering colour. Presidents, and Prime Ministers, in their sober suits, still like to see a red carpet rolled out for them when they pay a visit.

This dye became so famous in the ancient world that the Canaanites were called after the Greek word for the colour. They became known as 'Phoenicians', everywhere but among themselves. Even when they were scattered round the shores of the Mediterranean, they remember their homeland. To the end of their long history, they called themselves Canaanites.

Two Kings

I have said enough, I trust, about the Phoenicians to show that they were among the most interesting people in antiquity. It does not seem that they thought so themselves. They wrote no histories. The Greeks found the Greeks so fascinating that they not only wrote their history, they invented history itself. The Phoenicians did not raise obelisks like the Egyptians, or carve inscriptions on cliffs like the Assyrians and Persians. They were too busy making money and enjoying the good life. To know anything about them we have to piece together what their neighbours said about them or to dig with the spade in the scarce ruins of their cities and unearth the tombs of their kings. From that, we know that they had their ups and downs, like any other people, their triumphs and disasters. They did not vaunt the first, nor brood upon the second.

We do not know where they came from. By 3000 BC they were settled in the Lebanon: they may have been there always, they may have come from the hinterland. They were probably indistinguishable from other Semites, except for one thing. They took to the sea, a thing no other Semitic people was to do until the Arabs, and even these, though good sailors, greatly preferred dry land.

For the first thousand years or so, the Phoenicians were nothing very much. Two great civilizations overshadowed them, the Egyptian and the Minoan. The Egyptians were confirmed landlubbers, but the Minoans gloried in their mastery of the sea. They built a sea-empire, inside which the Phoenicians must have crept about in their boats in a very discreet and humble fashion.

Then came a happening which convulsed civilization, changing its course forever. What exactly it was, remains a mystery. Historians have called it the Time of Troubles, for there is evidence that everywhere in the Eastern Mediterranean was under pressure from invaders from the land-mass. The invaders were rough and destructive. The high and almost over-refined Minoan civilization went down under them. Great cities like Knossos were laid in ruins: the sea-empire disappeared. The Mediterranean was open.

The Phoenicians took their chance. They sailed the sea-routes, not to found another empire, but to indulge their more peaceable passion for trade. So far from making an empire, they did not even trouble to make a nation. Their cities prospered. Tyre, Sidon, and Byblos became rich. It would have been perfectly natural for the king of one of them to try to subdue the others. It was never done. Each city was content with what it had within its own walls and what its own ships brought home. It is tempting to think of how much misery and horror the world would have been saved if other peoples had possessed as much common-sense as the Phoenicians.

On the other hand, they were extremely irritating to their neighbours. To nations bordering their territories, they seemed smug. In fact, so much so that they drove one Hebrew into a burst of fury that gave rise to some of the most magnificent prose ever written. It has been preserved in the Bible. The prophet Ezekiel, after drawing a glowing picture of the wealth and ease of the King of Tyre, changes his tone and thunders out a prophecy of the utter destruction of the city which must have fallen gratefully on the ears of his Hebrew listeners, then, unfortunately, in exile:

"And the word of the Lord came to me, saying, Son of man. take up a lament-ation upon the King of Tyre.
And say to him: Thus saith the Lord God: 'Thou wast the seal of resemblance, full of wisdom and perfect in beauty. . . . Every precious stone was thy covering: the sardius, the topaz and the jasper, the chrysolite and the onyx and the beryl, the sapphire and the carbuncle, and the emerald. . . .
Thou wast perfect in thy ways from the day of thy creation, till iniquity was found in thee. By the multitude of thy merchandise, thy inner parts were filled with iniquity and thou hast sinned: and I cast thee out from the mountain of God and destroyed thee. . . . All that shall see thee among the nations shall be astonished at thee: thou art brought to nothing and thou shalt never be any more.'"

16 *This detail of a relief from Karnak (1504–1450 BC) is a record of exotic animals and plants brought back to Egypt from a Syrian campaign.*

He was right. Tyre was destroyed, but before that, it had long centuries of getting by. The Phoenicians had not a touch of heroism. They could fight if need be: Tyre withstood a thirteen-years siege by Nebuchadnezzar. But they much preferred not to. Every so often, their neighbours, who were their customers, conceived the idea of raiding the shop instead of paying for the goods. The first were the Egyptians. They conquered the Lebanon; it would seem that the Phoenicians put up little resistance, preferring to pay the tribute that the Pharaoh levied on them. The Assyrians did the same thing. The conquering king, Tiglathpileser I, has left us a record of what happened:

"At that time I marched along the side of Mount Lebanon, and to the Great Sea of the land of Amurru I went up. In the Great Sea I washed my weapons, and I made offerings unto the gods. The tribute of the kings of the seacoast, of the people of Tyre, Sidon, Byblos, Makhalata, Maisa, Kaisa, Amurru, and Aradus, which lies in the midst of the sea – silver, gold, lead, copper, vessels of bronze, garments made of brightly coloured wool, linen garments, a great monkey, and a small monkey, maple-wood, boxwood, and ivory, and a nahiru, a creature of the sea, I received as tribute from them, and they embraced my feet."

32

17 *Ramses III (1195–1164 BC) attacking a walled fortress manned by Syrian lancers; from a relief at Thebes.* ⟩

18 *Tribute being brought from Tyre to Assyria after Shalmaneser III's conquest (9th century BC).*

19 *A double-shekel from Sidon,* c. *450 BC, showing a warship under full sail.*

20, 21 *Representations of Phoenician galleys on coins from Aradus and Byblos.*

22 *This detail of Shalmaneser III's campaign in North Syria shows the impaled inhabitants of a Syrian town in the lower section.*

23 *The Dome of the Rock in Jerusalem is on the supposed site of Solomon's Temple and is also traditionally the spot of Abraham's sacrifice.*

There were, of course, kings of Tyre who lacked the usual Phoenician skill, or who were pricked by ambition. These led their cities into open revolts. They were always put down. But Tyre survived. Tributes were imposed and paid, but for all that, the Phoenicians got richer. Tyre's sister city of Sidon was at one time destroyed, only to rise again. It was the custom in those times for a conqueror to massacre a portion of the inhabitants of a rebellious city and sell the rest into slavery. This did not happen to the Phoenicians, for a reason which I shall explain.

But, before I do, I wish to give a picture of the friendly, not to say, sunny relations which this extraordinarily deft people maintained with a neighbour. It comes partly from the annals of Tyre, and partly from the Bible.

Hiram, King of Tyre, had known David, King of Judah, the David who had slain Goliath and danced naked in front of the Ark of the Lord. Hiram had been very fond of him, and when he heard that his son, Solomon, had acceded to the throne, he sent a delegation to congratulate him. In return, Solomon sent a delegation to Hiram. Through his ambassadors, he reminded Hiram that David, his friend, had always wished to build a Temple to the Lord, but was too preoccupied with wars to do it. So he had left the task to his son. All was now peaceful, and Solomon intended to do his duty to his father's memory. He would build a temple. For this, he needed wood from the cedars of Lebanon. He asked Hiram to supply it, since, he said, 'nobody can hew timber like the Phoenicians.' Hiram was delighted to be of service. Solomon was delighted in his turn. He would supply Hiram with twenty-thousand measures of wheat each year of the building and twenty measures of pure oil.

Not only were the Phoenicians good at tree-felling; they had developed formidable skills in building. Solomon welcomed the craftsmen and set them to work. A design for the Temple was needed. Solomon, with remarkable broadness of mind, adopted the plan of Hiram's temple in Tyre, in spite of the notorious abominations which went on in them. Thus, it came about that the Ark of the Lord, who had grown so angry at the sight of the Golden Calf, was set in a sanctuary built by idolaters. It was embellished with gold, and that came from Hiram, too.

The whole transaction was so successful that Solomon gave Hiram twenty villages in Galilee. But here a cloud passes over their friendship. Hiram inspected the villages. The annals of Tyre are blunt about what happened. 'But when Hiram went to them and looked them over, he was ill-pleased with the gift,' they say, 'and sent word to Solomon that he had no use for them.'

Yet even that contretemps was smoothed over. Gifts, in those days, were meant to be paid for, just as they were among the Greeks, as we learn from the *Iliad*. The Bible tells us that Hiram, swallowing his discontent, paid up one hundred and twenty talents of gold.

Now Solomon, as we know, had a high opinion of his intellectual abilities. He proposed to his friend, Hiram, that they should exchange riddles. If one of them could not answer them, he would have to pay a forfeit, and it is clear that

24 *Overleaf: an aerial view of the city of Jerusalem.*

the payment was to be on a kingly scale. Hiram agreed. Solomon sent the first set. Hiram had to admit that he could not answer them. He paid the forfeit, but it nearly bankrupted him. However, he was not to be beaten so easily. He applied himself to the questions again (or applied to some bright brain among his subjects) and he found the answers. He, in his turn, sent riddles to Solomon. Solomon, for all his wisdom, could not find the solutions. Apparently, there was no genius among the Jews as there was among the Phoenicians. Solomon had to admit defeat. He paid back Hiram's money and a large sum in addition for his own forfeit.

The relationship of the two men is a pleasant picture, and much more pleasant to contemplate than the splenetic invective of Ezekiel. But the prophet was right in the end. Tyre passed safely through the dominion of the Assyrians, the Babylonians, the Persians, the Macedonians and the Romans, maintaining its wealth and its skills intact. When Cleopatra dressed up, it was in the diaphanous silks that only Tyre could weave. Yet in the end, Tyre was destroyed, exactly as Ezekiel had said. It was done by the Arabs. But that was in AD 1291, and, by that time, the prophet had been more than one thousand and eight hundred years in his grave.

25 A Punic stele, c. 4th century BC, from Carthage. ⟩

26 Overleaf: view of Leptis Magna, looking over the theatre proscenium towards the sea.

Sailors

The main reason that the Phoenicians were spared massacre and slavery was that they were excellent sailors. A conquering king could order his army to march across deserts and scale mountains. But sooner or later, he would come to the shores of the Mediterranean. If he wanted to go further, he must hire boats. Warfare, until the time of Alexander the Great and his father's invention of the phalanx, was a simple affair. It consisted of slashing about with swords, casting javelins, drawing bows, or slinging stones. These are things which can be taught a boy in a month. Even in our own more complicated times, it takes only ninety days to turn a raw civilian into a competent soldier.

The warriors of the Egyptians, the Assyrians, the Babylonians and the Persians were basically mobs. The art of warfare was to have a bigger mob than the enemy. You kept your mob from sensibly running away when the battle commenced by bribery, the promise of loot and rape, or, ultimately, by threatening to kill every tenth man if your troops proved cowards. But in a storm at sea, there is no point in throwing a percentage of sailors overboard. You are in the hands of the captain and the crew, and your only hope lies in the fact that if they drown you, they know they will drown themselves as well. Moreover, you cannot make sailors in a matter of days. In those times, when there were no maps and no lighthouses, it was a skill that had to be passed from father to son. It still is, in the Mediterranean. On the northern shores of Italy is a small town with a tiny harbour called Camoglie. For centuries it has produced sailors. They still sail the ships of the world.

Why were the Phoenicians, alone among the Semites, such good sailors? Their homeland, of course, bordered the Mediterranean. But so did that of the

Etruscans, who sailed boats but only with the greatest caution, hugging the coasts. Rome was virtually on the coast, but the Romans were the first to admit that they were appallingly clumsy on the water. The Greeks, with their inlets and islands, learned early to sail boats. But even they greatly admired the Phoenicians, especially for their discipline when aboard, something which was lacking in the Greek navy. There is no hard and fast historical answer to why the Phoenicians were so good. That being so, perhaps I can permit myself a little speculation. Two other nations have proved themselves masters of navigation – the English and the Dutch. Both were, and are, countries passionately addicted to trade. They are both nations of shopkeepers, as were the Phoenicians. Perhaps there is some connection. Traders are pragmatists, and sailing a boat is a very pragmatical business.

The Phoenicians had three types of boats. There was a long, lean ship, a little like the ships of the Vikings, which was used for soldiers who acted as mariners to protect the merchant fleet. This was made up of bigger ships, very full-bellied. Both types were propelled by rowers equipped with long-bladed oars, or, when the wind was favourable, by a single sail in the form of a trapezoid. There were also little round boats, used for punting about on short journeys. The big ships had an upper deck above the rowers, and, if we can rely on the Bible, a cabin furnished in great luxury. Later in their history, the Phoenicians had the triremes with which we are all familiar, and it may even be that they themselves invented them.

Apart from their discipline, the merit of the Phoenician sailors lay in their great skill in maneuvre. At this, they were unbeatable, and since a naval battle leaned heavily on this art, they were formidable opponents, especially when it came to ramming. The Romans learned this to their cost in their first battle, when they lost their fleet. Such was the renown of the Phoenicians that the Romans had no thought of matching them, in, so to speak, their own territory. With much ingenuity, the Romans turned the sea-battle into a fight on land. To do this, the Romans equipped their new fleet with gangplanks fitted with grappling hooks. These they allowed to fall on the Phoenician ships and then they swarmed aboard, deciding the issue in a hand-to-hand fight. From that fact alone, we can see how good the Phoenician sailors were.

46

They sailed only in the daytime. Each night they had to find an anchorage. Further, they did not sail in the wintertime, a practice which brought out another aspect of the character of this remarkable people. When the autumn equinox came round, they pulled in their boats, beached them at some deserted spot, and turned themselves into farmers. They tilled the soil and grew the food they needed, until spring came round, and they resumed their voyages.

They were astonishing voyages. One of their captains, called Hanno, sailed all along the north coast of Africa, rounded the hump that juts out into the Atlantic, and finished up, safe and sound, in the Gulf of Guinea. We have a report of the voyage. It was very peaceful: the inhabitants fled to the interior at the sight of them. Another did even more. He circumnavigated the whole African continent. Yet another, Himilco, sailed through the Straits of Gibraltar, rounded Spain, passed the Bay of Biscay, and arrived at Brittany.

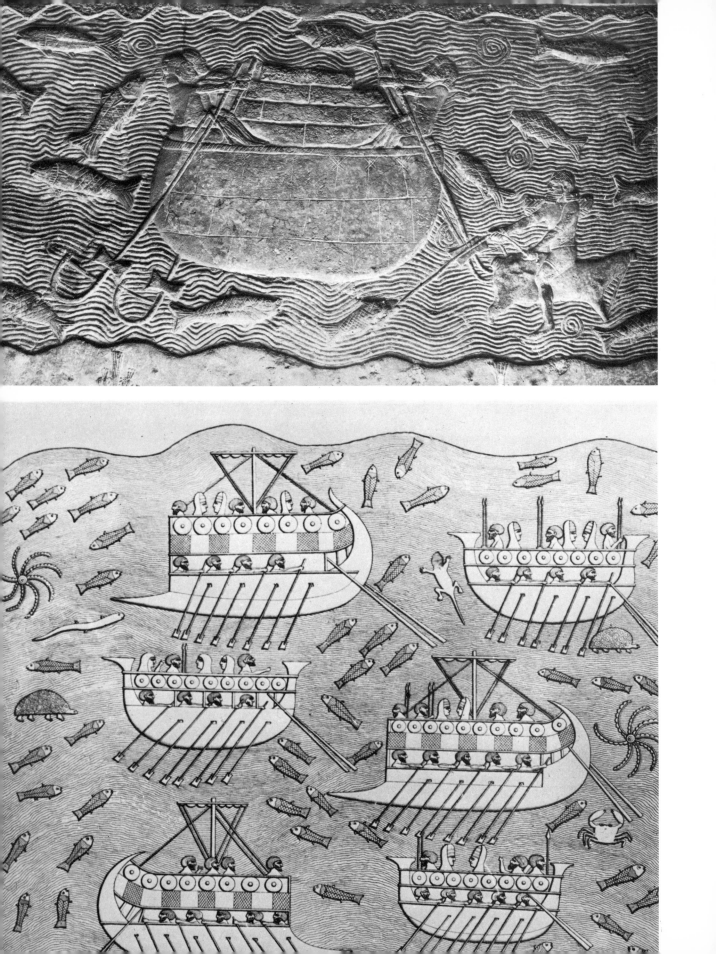

28–31 *Phoenician sea power. Above left, an Assyrian relief, 8th century BC, showing a skin-covered coracle similar to the small round boats of the Phoenicians. Left, drawing of an Assyrian relief in which two of the three Phoenician boat types are shown. Above, the Phoenician warship in this fragment confirms the drawing left. Right, a Roman merchant vessel on a Phoenician sarcophagus from Sidon.*

Settlements

We are told so remorselessly nowadays that the world is over-crowded, that it is difficult for us to imagine a group of mariners settling down for the winter in some spot and resting there, undisturbed, till the spring. But in the eighth century BC, the Mediterranean was an empty place. Parts of it still are. I remember Prince Karim, the Aga Khan, telling me of the excitement he felt when, one day, in North Sardinia, he and a group of friends came across mile after mile of deserted coastline. They bounded from rock to rock, shouting with glee, like boys. Then and there, they decided to found a settlement, which has now become the Costa Smeralda and a resort for the rich.

Just so, the Phoenicians settled. Like the Aga Khan, they bought their land, should anybody claim it, and again like him, no doubt for a very low price. Prince Karim told me how struck he was by the indifference of such inhabitants that he came across. They neither resented his coming nor thought it would make much difference to them. By and large, they were just amused.

The Phoenicians emigrated to find peace and quiet. Their homeland, the Lebanon, was the focal point of vast empires. Armies constantly trampled through it on their way to war. Distant monarchs levied taxes, which, if never ruinous, were still taxes, and they are something everyone can do without. So great numbers of them left, to found new cities. But they had no touch of the empire-builder about them: nor were they far-seeing colonists coming to found new kingdoms. They remained simply merchants who found their home-towns had grown inconvenient and crowded. When they went away, they left their hearts behind them. Some who went from Tyre founded Carthage, a name which merely meant, in their language, 'the new town'. Carthage grew bigger and

< 32 *The advantageous harbour of Carthage is clear in this air view of the city.*

33, 34 *Remnants of Carthage :*
jewelry, and a female bust which
shows signs of Hellenization.

52

35, 36 *Two masks found at Carthage.*

richer even than Tyre, but the Carthaginians always considered themselves citizens of Tyre. Each year they sent a pious tribute to their homeland. They even chose cities which resembled those of the cities they had left. Tyre and Sidon were built on promontories, Tyre being virtually an island. A promontory is easily defended. It is washed by the sea on two sides and thus provides two harbours.

The Phoenicians settled along the northern coasts of Africa. They settled in Spain, beyond the Pillars of Hercules, at Gades, which is now Cadiz. They settled in Sardinia. It was once thought that all these settlements had disappeared. But in recent years, one of them has been discovered and dug up. It is called Tharros: it is one of the least known and least visited ruins in the Mediterranean, which is strange, because it is an ancestor of Wall Street and Mincing Lane.

37 *A Phoenician gold bracelet with the palmette motif, 7th or 6th century BC, from Tharros (Sardinia).*

38, 39 *These two necklaces of various kinds of beads, with gold trimmings and mountings, also came from Tharros, 6th century BC.*

Tharros lies at one end of the great bay of Oristano, a sickle of sandy beach backed by dunes. There is no modern town, or even village, anywhere near it. In summer, there are scattered holiday-makers: in winter there is nobody at all.

The ruins of Tharros are yellow and white. They sprawl along the promontory like the skeleton of some sea monster. The roads are narrow and steep, running downwards to stop abruptly at the sea. The houses are small, cramped up one against the other, with here and there a narrow alley, like the Casbah of a Moroccan town today. You wander among them, looking in vain for some plan, but there is none. The houses have no decoration, being little more than boxes, with, sometimes, a rough mosaic floor. It would seem, at first, that its inhabitants had no taste for art.

But they had one, a merchant's taste. A necropolis has been unearthed. In the tombs was found exquisite jewellery. One bracelet, covered in a pattern worked in tiny beads of gold, is a masterpiece of the jeweller's craft.

Something much grimmer has been unearthed. In the very heart of the city is a high, stone platform. Around its edges or walls, at its far end, are the remains of a shrine. This is the temple, and enough of it remains for us to know what it looked like.

A great flight of slab-like steps led up to it, with walls on each side. At the top of the broad steps, a narrower flight led up, sheltered by the walls and roof of the sanctuary. Inside this sanctuary stood the statue of the god. It is not possible to stand upon these stones without a shudder.

The Tophets

The deities who lived in temples such as these were often benign. Each city had its own god or goddess, sometimes two or three. In Byblos, there was El, a sort of heavenly governor or lord mayor, who ran the city in return for prayers and sacrifices, keeping its citizens safe and prosperous. There was also Baalat, a comfortable goddess who represented Mother Earth, treated with such respect that she was referred to by her title – Baalat means 'Lady'. So, for that matter, was the more romantic figure of Adonis, for the name means 'my lord'. He had a story behind him. He was a beautiful youth, much beloved by the goddess whom the Greeks later called Aphrodite. But he was killed. Aphrodite went down into Hell to plead for his return to the light of day. Some stories say that she succeeded. Adonis was resurrected, but some Phoenicians (no doubt born sceptics) believed that he stayed dead. Baalat and El are forgotten, but Adonis is not. He is remembered every Good Friday, here in Rome, the heart of Christianity. For the hours which Jesus spent in the tomb, each of Rome's numberless churches has a side-chapel smothered in flowers. It is called 'the sepulchre' and men and women journey from one to another, saying a prayer. On the floors of these sepulchres are small pots in which grows a sort of feathery, fresh-looking grass, symbolizing the return of Christ from the harrowing of Hell. They are called 'Gardens of Adonis'.

Tyre had Melqart, a travelling god, for wherever the Tyrians went, they set up a temple to him: there was even one in far-off Spain, at Gades. Sidon had a goddess, Astarte. She, too, travelled to Carthage, where she changed her name to Tanit. The veil which shrouded her statue was considered to have magical powers to protect the city, just as in Rome, the Vestal Virgin jealously guarded a

56

40 *Alabaster cult statue of Astarte, a Phoenician work, 7th-6th century BC, from the Granada area.* >

41 *Relief of Melqart on a stele from Tyre (Lebanon).*

42, 43 *Melqart riding on a sea-horse, obverse of a shekel from Tyre, c. 380 BC. The reverse bears an owl of the Egyptian type similar to the shekel from Tyre (illustration 15) of nearly a century before.*

44 *The sign of the god Tanit, a mosaic from Sabratha (Libya).*

number of secret objects – they are still secret for we do not know what they are – which were thought to have the same effects.

Astarte was gratified by the sacrifice of vegetables and small animals, but particularly pleased with the less onerous (but perhaps just as expensive) sacrifice of semen. She rejoiced in copulation in the indiscriminate manner which, millennia later, has now been revived among the progressive young. There were female devotees who had sex with the worshipper. There were 'temple boys', who also enjoyed popularity, to judge from the number of votive carvings dedicated to them which archaeologists have found.

Astarte was a generous goddess. Her statues had bare breasts, with holes in her nipples. These (it has been thought) were stuffed with wax. During the ceremonies in her honour, the heat in the temple would increase, from the tapers, the lamps, and the heat of the worshippers' bodies. The wax would melt, and Astarte would pour forth milk. Even that harmless piece of priestly deception has survived. In the Cathedral of Naples there is preserved a flask of the blood of the martyred Saint Januarius. It is normally solid. Twice a year the Cathedral is jam-packed. Innumerable candles are lit. The heat rises to a degree (as I can testify) almost insupportable for one who is not a Neapolitan. At a certain point, the blood liquefies. A great shout of rejoicing goes up. Whenever I have heard it, my thoughts have gone back to Sidon. Just such a shout must have echoed round the temple when Astarte gushed forth in a sign that all would be well.

The Mediterranean is a very old place: and such thoughts are constantly on one's mind. Unfortunately they are not always so pleasant.

I was conducting a search for the Phoenicians along its shores, so I went from Tharros to Carthage, the 'new city' the Tyrians had founded. There was nothing to see, at least above ground. The Romans had decreed that it should be destroyed, and they had done it with Roman thoroughness. I was shown around some columns and walls, but these were Roman baths, built on a plan to please Romans.

The modern town of Tunis has taken the place of Carthage and I went to its most modern suburb, Salammbo. It has neatly asphalted roads, lined with villas in the contemporary style, each with its garden. The suburb was designed for

45 *Precinct of Tanit at Salammbo, Carthage, 8th-4th century BC.*

high-grade civil servants, successful businessmen and the like. It is very reassuring and comfortable. It is the improbable setting for the grimmest monument left to us by the ancient world.

In what appears at first sight to be yet another commuter's garden is a large hole in the ground. I was led down this by some steps. Around me was a great mass of burial urns. Some were square stone boxes with a pyramid on top. Others more fanciful were in the shape of little houses, with columns at the door. I descended through floor after floor of these until I came to the bottom.

Here were the ruins of a shrine or perhaps a chapel. It had been dedicated, in the second millennium before Christ, to Tanit (who was, as I have said, Astarte) and the god Baal Hammon. The amiable humanity of Astarte, with her sex and milk, was not to be found here. This was the place where, whenever great

60

46 *A Phoenician burial jar, containing the bones of a child sacrifice, from Salammbo.*

danger threatened the city, the people brought infants-in-arms and had a priest kill them in front of the goddess and burn them in a holy brazier. The children had to be their own, born of their loins. If a father, unable to bring himself to make the sacrifice, bought some slave-child and offered him up (and some did), the goddess rained calamities upon him and his fellow-citizens, to teach them a lesson.

The bones of the victim were reverently gathered and placed in the urns, with an inscription nearby to mark the deed. Some of the urns are open, and the little bones can be seen.

The rite was so horrifying that for a long time historians were unwilling to believe that it ever took place. The writers of the Old Testament called these places 'tophets', which is the name they still go by. It was thought they were the invention of enemies and rivals of the Canaanites. Scholars searched through Latin literature written at a time when Roman propaganda was at its bitterest against the Carthaginians, and were relieved when they found no mention of 'tophets'.

But they are there. They have been dug up. The fact that the Romans did not denounce them was due to the fact that they knew the Carthaginians late in the day, when the custom was at last dying out. The Romans utterly destroyed Carthage, driving a plough over it. But they did not destroy the tophet, presumably because they did not know it was there.

There were tophets elsewhere: in Tharros, in Tyre, in Sidon, and perhaps in every city. There is not much to be said in extenuation. At least it is pleasant to know the poor did not bear the burden. The children of the noblest families were preferred. The ceremony was performed only in times of the greatest danger, and it was therefore not very frequent. Then, too, the story of some monstrous metal god called Moloch, with movable arms that fed the infant into a furnace in its belly is, indeed, a piece of propaganda. 'Moloch' is a correlation of the word 'molk' and 'molk' was the name of the ceremony, not of a god. 'Moloch' did not exist.

But there can be no doubts about the rest. There is even a funerary stele with an incised carving of a priest. He is dressed in a long tunic. He is shaven bald: and he holds a child in the crook of his arm as he takes it towards its death.

Climbing back out of the tophet into the sunlight, I recalled that we, too, kill children when we feel our country is threatened, so frequently that we might almost call it part of our way of life. We do it by aerial bombing, which is not so ceremonious, and not so superstitious. But it kills a lot more of them.

47 A priest carrying a child for sacrifice in a tophet; a Punic stele in Tunis. ⟩

The Punic Wars

I must now tell of the great wars between the Phoenicians of Carthage and the Romans, but I intend to be very brief. Wars were very interesting to our fathers and forefathers. They thought they were pretty fine things. They brought out the best in a people. They produced military geniuses who were considered the apex of a culture.

I have never been able to feel this since the day I visited the shrine of one of the greatest military geniuses who ever lived. It was in the little town of Ajaccio, in Corsica. Napoleon was born there: a vast and exceedingly ugly shrine has been erected to him. I visited it. It was the nineteen-fifties. On the day I went there the floor of the shrine was covered with coffins. There must have been a hundred of them, all the same, except for the names on their labels. I was being conducted around by the caretaker, an elderly woman, in a state of profound depression. I asked her what the coffins contained. She sat down on one of them, and told me. They were the dead from the war in Indo-China.

She was bitterly opposed to it, to the point of speaking through tears of anger. I need not record what she said. We have all heard it ten thousand times since, from the measured voices in the Senate of the United States, to the young shouting in the streets right around the world. It will be sufficient to say that since that day at the shrine to Napoleon, I have never had much taste for generals.

It would seem that the Carthaginians began by behaving in a thoroughly Phoenician manner. In 348 BC they signed a treaty with the Romans promising to keep their traders out of Roman territory, and what Rome considered territory vital to her safety.

But Carthage grew enormously successful. In due course, she felt that she had to take recourse to wars in order to protect her commercial interests. She did not do very well, but sufficiently well to frighten the Romans, who conceived the idea that the Carthaginians intended, in some distant future, to make war on them. There is no evidence that the Carthaginians had any such idea. But the Romans were concerned with their prestige, especially in the eyes of their allies.

So Rome went to war, a bitter one which lasted one hundred and eighteen years. The details can be found in any history book. They are the usual details. Victories were won against tremendous odds, gargantuan blunders were made, heroes arose on both sides, men died like flies.

Inevitably, a military genius arose, unexpectedly from the side of the Phoenicians. We all know his name, Hannibal, largely because he led elephants over the Alps, a mighty feat, only spoiled by the fact that they all died.

Hannibal was so near success that he came within sight of Rome. He pitched his camp on a plain up in the hills that overlooks the city. It is now a favourite spot for Sunday picnics, and nobody, I am glad to say, has ever thought of raising a monument to the mighty man.

He lost his war because the Carthaginians back home grew tired of the cost of it, and the loss of life. They refused, or procrastinated, when he asked for recruits.

The end of it all was that the Romans invaded Africa, took Carthage, sacked it, burned it, and destroyed it.

But they by no means destroyed the Phoenicians. The Romans went on to build the biggest empire the world had seen. The Phoenicians, having learned their lesson, quietly returned to their previous paths of peace and trade. Centuries later they had their revenge. A Phoenician boy, born in the town of Leptis Magna, came to Rome to complete his education under the masters of his people. He learned his lessons so well that he became their ruler.

He was an efficient emperor, who throughout his life maintained an attitude of contempt and indifference to the Romans himself. He has left behind him two mementoes: the magnificent ruins of the great city he made of Leptis Magna, and the reputation of being the man who began the decline and fall of the Roman Empire. Even the Romans called it 'the Punic revenge'.

48 *This aerial view of Leptis Magna shows the theatre, the Chalcidium (right) and the market (top right).*

Leptis Magna

I would recommend any student of the past to save up Leptis Magna to the last. As a sight, as an experience, there is nothing to equal it: it satisfies completely. I have seen most of the other great monuments. The Parthenon is very fine, but coming back to it, time and again over the years, I find that its very perfection becomes boring. After twenty years of looking at the ruins of Rome, I have come to agree with the most ignorant tourist – they are sadly battered. To know what Rome was really like, I nowadays prefer to pick up Martial or Juvenal, and take them off to bed to read in the Roman night. Before I stopped counting, I had made thirty visits to Pompeii and Herculaneum. They are both miracles, but provincial miracles. The antique world was not as narrow as these. Knossos is more of a puzzle than anything else, made forever unsolvable by Sir Arthur Evans treating it as his private property (which it was), and making it over to suit his fancy. Leptis Magna is perfect. It has splendour: it is as complete as any reasonable man could wish for: the restorers have been happily hampered by political convulsions and lack of funds: above all, you can walk in its ruins for days on end, as I have done, and see nobody. I say this in 1972, and I am only too well aware that, in a decade, I can sound ridiculous. Still, I do not think the Libyans will make any serious attempt to develop it, as the word goes, for a long time to come. They are too absorbed in their newly-discovered oil.

To see it, one must go to Tripoli, the most repellently ugly city on the shores of the Mediterranean. One must put up with the loquacious and boozing oil-men: one must pay oil-men's prices. But that need last for one night only.

It was oil of another sort which attracted the Romans and led them to the conquest of Carthage and then of all North Africa. One drives out in the early morning on the road to Homs, with the sea on the left and grey-green olive groves on one's right. Then, later, searching fingers of sand, like little flows of golden lava, begin to snake between the trees and even spill upon the road. This is the sand of the desert, the sand which buried Leptis Magna after the Romans had gone, both those Romans of the Western Empire and those of Byzantium, and after the Vandals had torn down as much of the city as they had time and energy to do. They knocked down a number of the marble and sandstone columns, but after that Leptis was left in peace, to sleep and steep in the African sun, under its blanket of sand.

Rome was mainly destroyed by Renaissance Popes, who vastly admired the classical buildings, had them meticulously measured by their architects, then tore them down to use the stone and marble. It is recorded that one contractor took 28,000 cart-loads of stone from the Colosseum, and, as I have ascertained by a close inspection, the columns of the portico of St Peter's are Roman remains. The two guarding the main portico door, which all the world sees when the Pope gives his Easter blessing, are even patched.

Leptis escaped this, more or less. Some columns were taken away during the centuries. There are some in the church of Saint-Germain-des-Près in Paris: others can be found on the royal estate at Windsor in England. But these were minor robberies. Leptis, now the sand is slowly being dug away, remains the most complete city which has come down to us from the ancient world.

From the first glimpse of it, its sheer size overwhelms you. It was founded by the Phoenicians in the tenth century BC, and, as was their custom, they chose a promontory that sheltered a harbour. But it grew mightily, spreading along the shores, like a river of stone. It was built of marble and sandstone, and the centuries have turned it into a city of amber – from the patina which has spread over its stones. Sometimes, when the sun is right, and when it is seen from the sea, it looks like a legendary city built of gold.

There is still sand in its streets: it creeps back almost as fast as the archaeologists dig it out. In the sands grow dark, low shrubs in wide swathes where the spade has not yet struck, a perfect setting for the ruins, setting them off, but not obscuring them.

49, 50 *Above, the market place at Leptis Magna. Below, a view of the west apse of the Severan Basilica at Leptis Magna.* ⟩

There are only vestiges of walls, still under excavation. You enter by a great arch, standing by itself. It was set up on the orders of the boy from Leptis who had become Emperor, Septimius Severus. It is tempting to think that it was built to commemorate his returning in pomp and majesty to his native town, but we have no certain evidence that he ever went back. But we do know that he gave orders that the town be beautified on an Imperial scale. This arch is the first proof we meet that his orders were obeyed. It remains one of the most important monuments of Roman art.

It has four entrances, flanked by elegant Corinthian columns. These were crowned by pointed, triangular cornices, heavily carved, and which have been found. They lent the arch a bold, thrusting liveliness, and break, successfully, the rules of classical architecture. Nobody can tell where this new idea came from, but perhaps it came from this very region. To this day, houses in the interior have decorations very like them, but much smaller. They are intended to ward off the evil eye.

Beside the arch, buried in the sand, were found huge reliefs. They are remark- ably well-preserved (they are now in the Bardo Museum in Tunis). They show the Emperor Septimius Severus, with his two sons, Commodus and Gaeta, performing various ceremonies: he is riding in a triumphal chariot, sacrificing in a temple with his head covered in a veil, as ritual prescribed. There is an extremely vivid portrayal of the sacrificial bull being slaughtered amid a great crowd of courtiers, all rendered with brilliant realism. So is the Emperor. He has a broad face, with large, expressive eyes that are turned upwards in a haughty stare over the heads of his subjects. He is heavily bearded, but that does not conceal thick, fleshy lips with a sceptical downward turn. It is the exact rendering of the man who once remarked that he had seen everything and done everything and it was all worth nothing much.

He also has high, rounded, African cheekbones, such as can still be seen in Libya. It is an important fact, as I shall show when I tell of his birth and his life.

The arch gives on to a paved street, lined with mounds which are still not excavated, but which contain houses. This long perspective ends in another arch, a very simple one, with a rounded top, built by the Emperor Tiberius, in whose reign Jesus died. On each side of this lie the principal ruins of Leptis.

⟨ *51, 52 Above, hunting wild animals, 3rd century AD mosaic from Algeria. Below, antelope being loaded on to a ship, 3rd-4th century AD mosaic from Piazza Armerina, Sicily.*

72

53–56 *The Arch of Septimius Severus, Leptis Magna, c. AD 200. Opposite, a reconstruction of the Arch. Above, a detail of the relief showing a sacrificial ceremony. Below left, a triangular cornice from the Arch. Below right, a detail of the relief showing Septimius Severus and his two sons, Commodus and Geta.*

57 View along a paved street to the Arch of Trajan, Leptis Magna.

We pass under another arch, this time built by Trajan. It, too, has columns, but the contrast between it and the flamboyant arch of Septimius Severus is so striking that I have several times walked back along the road to compare them. Here, with Trajan, all is classical, restrained and orderly. Even the mouldings of the bases of the column tell different tales. Those of the Trajan arch are almost delicate: those of the other are heavy and bold. Seventy-six years separate the two reigns and it is clear that a profound change had come over taste. Walking between them, I felt it was not too much to detect the first sign of that unbridled wilfulness which, as soon as Severus died, was to sweep over the Roman Empire and reduce it to chaos.

But we must not lose sight of the fact that this was a Semitic people, living in a town founded for trade and growing rich by trade. It was an independent Punic city, save for a brief period under a Numidian king, Masinissa, until it was finally subdued by the Romans in 23 BC. But for all their Roman masters, Leptis was built and adorned by its citizens. They left their names inscribed on stone to remind us, and the list of them tells their story: Iddibal, Ithymbal, Annobal, Ammicar, Balithon, Boncarth, Muthumbal, Bodmelqart, Himilcho, and Byrycth. Men, that is, of Punic stock.

It is therefore fit and proper that we should go straight to the heart of the city, which, inevitably, was the Market Place.

It is a great paved space supporting a forest of columns, over a hundred of them, and many complete. As befits a place of such importance, it was approached by an elaborate portico, and securely walled round, like a fortress. Once inside these walls, all is charm and lightness. A columned walk ran round all four walls. In the centre were two octagonal pavilions, the roof supported on the outside by columns, and in the middle by a second, circular pavilion, pierced by arches. There can be no doubt that these were the auricle and ventricle of Leptis Magna: elaborate monuments to the most distinguished and deserving citizens were erected beside them. Today, only the bases remain standing, stone models of a four-way arch, on which were placed honorific chariots made of gleaming bronze. On one of them was carved a more direct and blunt reminder of where all that hard-won money had come from – two excellent reliefs of ships, one with a sail and one without.

58 *An inscription from the theatre at Leptis Magna, showing the name Annobal.*

There is an even more impressive reminder at the far end. Some of the stalls from which trade was done have survived. These consist of marble walls, supported, as though by buttresses, by beautifully rendered carvings of dolphins.

Merchants can be honest, provided they are kept honest. Here, in the market place, is the block of stone which controlled the weights, also of stone. There are depressions into which the weights had to fit with accuracy. Another stone has lines upon it that helped in converting one linear measure into another, as useful to foreigners as the currency tables we carry round with us today on our travels.

Even the hangers-on who frequent every market place have left a memorial – the porters, the errand boys, the idlers ready to snatch a tip or two for some light service. On a stone step are the holes which they used for playing some game to pass the moments when business was slack.

From the market, it is only a few steps to the place where the tired businessman relaxed, the theatre. The structure of the classical theatre is so well-known that it scarcely needs describing. There is a semi-circle of stone seats, a space in front of the stage, a raised stone platform and a permanent setting with three entrances and a profusion of pillars. There are a great number of them round the Mediter-

76

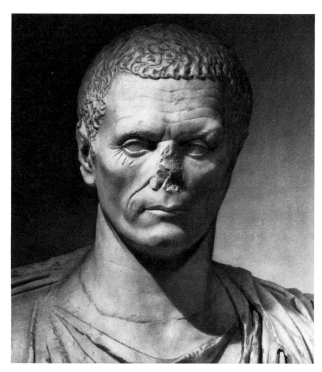

ranean. To any actor, and to any producer, they breathe 'theatre'. That has been their misfortune. For to any tourist board, they also breathe 'money' and, what is more, a solution to that vexing problem of what the tourist is to do in the evening.

So, each summer, classical plays are put on. Since you cannot charge very high prices for sitting on stone or wooden seats, the actors are second-rate. Since we have not the least idea of how the Chorus of a classical play behaved, the girls and boys of the local dance academy are called up to prance about in various postures, thought by the producer, on no basis whatever, to be Greek. Music is added, also very Greek, though not a single fragment of Greek music has survived. The performances are given at night because the producers cannot tear themselves away from electric light, although all classical performances were given in the daytime. The result has about as much connection with antiquity as a Coronation Procession put on at the Radio City Music Hall in New York would have with the history of the British Monarchy.

When all this started, I was inclined to consider it harmless, and sometimes quite funny. Now I am not so sure. The first problem was that it is a dangerous

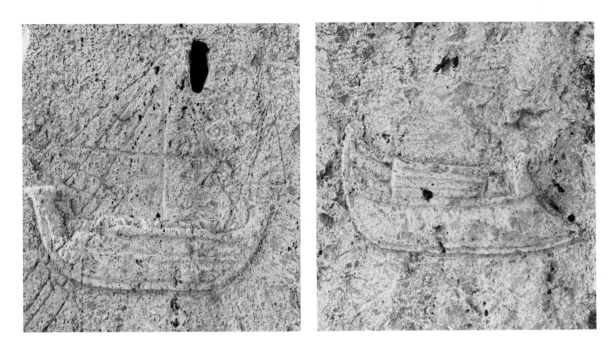

60–64 In the Market Place at Leptis Magna. Above, reliefs of a sailing boat and a cargo vessel. Below, counters with dolphin supports. Opposite above, incised linear measure on a block of stone. Opposite below, standard volume measures.

65 *The remains of the theatre at Leptis Magna.*

thing to stumble about ruins in the dark. Tourists must be protected from twisting an ankle or breaking a leg. The ruins, *ergo*, must be made rather less ruinous. A few slabs here, a few blocks there ('it *must* have been like this') and the place is made safe. The stage, too, though picturesque, is inconvenient and not to the modern taste in scene design. A column moved here, one set up there ('well, it belongs, doesn't it?'), and the producer gets his effects much better. Loose stones lying about are an impediment. Moving them a few feet can do no harm. Actors

80

dislike suddenly disappearing down holes in the stage, or elsewhere. Re-paving ('with the same stone the Romans used, mind you') is called for.

Thus, over the years, I have watched theatres like those of Ostia and Taormina being spruced up like a child going to a party. At Ostia they have even added a brand new and terribly 'Roman' foyer, fitted with a bar. I have seen the theatre at Taormina defiled with a giant panoramic screen suitable for the projection of films in Todd-AO. Loudspeakers, with their heavy cables, are expensive to install and dismount. It is better to leave them there, driving, of course, a few clamps in here and there to keep everything shipshape during the winter. As I write these words, I learn that, for a tourist show in the Roman Forum, the Cloaca Maxima has been wired for sound.

This has not happened at Leptis Magna. When the archaeologists cleared it from the sand, they found that a number of its columns had been thrown down, whether by an earthquake or an invader, it was difficult to say. But they had fallen in their places and could be safely re-erected. Some statues were also discovered. They were not carried off to the museums (though there would be reason in doing so) but, with great good sense, they were put back on their pedestals. The theatre is wonderfully complete, without faking. No producer has felt the itch to produce 'his' Sophocles there, and never will. Leptis is too remote to attract an audience, except, perhaps, of camel-drivers.

It is down by the shore, so that spectators in the top rows got a view of the Mediterranean. The stone rows descend to a wall, beyond which is a curved platform for the chairs of the chief men of Leptis.

In front of this is a semi-circular space, with the base of an altar in the middle. Beyond this rises the stage, fifty yards long and nine yards wide, quite untouched since the day it was discovered. Behind this, again, rises the *scaena*, the permanent background to the performance.

All classical stages had a very elaborate *scaena*, on which the architects lavished ornamentation to a degree that would not have been permitted them outside a theatre. That of Leptis is exceptionally elaborate. Basically, the *scaena* had to provide three doors. This requirement has been developed to make three curved apses, set about with columns. It is a highly successful design. In most other theatres the *scaena* was made an abrupt wall, like the lowered front curtain in our own theatres. Here the apses echo the great curve of the seats, binding the two parts of the building together.

Two screens, on each side of the stage, concentrated the spectator's attention on the action. Against these stood statues that gaze at the audience with remark-ably dramatic effect. The statue of the Dioscuros which remains on the site is a powerful piece of carving, done, it is thought, either in Rome or more probably in Greece, and transported here. Herms and busts complete the decoration.

66 Statue of Dioscuros in the theatre at Leptis Magna. ⟩

67 Roman mosaic of mimes, musicians and dancers.

The tired businessman of Leptis was, we may be sure, well catered to. On great occasions the great tragedies would have been performed: at other times, there would be the comedies of Plautus and Terence, in which the citizens would see themselves portrayed on the stage, usually without flattery. The performance of any play, whether tragedy or comedy, was utterly unlike anything we see today. For one thing, the actors, who wore masks, usually faced the audience. They could, if they wished, turn away, but the principal speeches were delivered frontally. All depended on two things: the beauty of the actor's declamation, and his gestures. In the declamation, clearness was everything: Vitruvius remarks, like a schoolmaster teaching Latin today, that the case-endings of words must not be mumbled.

Stranger still to us would be the Roman custom of having a flute-player on the stage. At crucial moments and in big speeches, he would approach the actor and underline his words with music. When we combine in our imagination the highly-trained, melodious voice of the actor, booming through the mask (he did not necessarily change his voice when taking a female part), the beauty of the gestures which were able to convey every emotion, and the sound of the flute, we can see that the stage must have had many gripping moments.

84

68 *Roman mosaic representing theatrical masks.*

There was less exacting fare. Companies of mimes toured the Empire and were immensely popular. They wore no masks: they often improvised (though texts were sometimes written for them) and their humour was low. They were dressed in a hood which could be drawn over their heads, or flung back. Beneath this was a simple tunic to which was attached a leather phallus, which, by means of a string, could be erected at a suitable point in the stories they told. Their favourite themes were adultery and homosexuality, but they varied these with topical allusions, often of a biting nature. In a commercial city like Leptis, it is easy to see that the mimes would be very welcome.

69 The Hadrianic Baths, dedicated AD 126–27, at Leptis Magna. ⟩

The Basilica

There is a fine view of Leptis from the top row of the theatre, and it is a view of columns, row upon row of them, stretching out into the distance. We nowadays are accustomed to a city being made of boxes, enormous like New York, small like Paris. It seems, at first, that there are too many columns in Leptis, too many porticoes, too many columned walks down the streets. But it is this which makes Leptis an instructive ruin. Columns fall down easily: once down, they are simple to cut up. In all the other cities that antiquity has left us, this has happened to a degree. Chance may have preserved the columns of a temple, but it rarely has spared the porticoes that surrounded it. They were, however, a vital part of any town built in the time of the Greeks and the Romans. Their importance has never, to my knowledge, been explained. I shall now attempt to do so.

Permit me, for a moment, to return to Rome. The climate of the Mediterranean is mild and sunny but it has days of what the Romans still call 'wickedness'. It may rain in torrents; sharp winds can blow; the summer sun can become too fierce to bear: every five years or so, there will be snow. None of these patches of bad weather lasts very long – a few days, and it is over. But because the weather is generally so gentle, they are felt, and disliked, all the more. A Roman comments more about the weather than even a Londoner.

For some years, I lived within a few steps of the Pantheon, the great round temple restored by Hadrian, and the only complete monument in the city. This has a portico, still covered by the original roof, which is supported by enormous columns, eight along the front, with two more rows behind them. Underneath there is ample space to stroll.

⟨ 70 *The Basilica at Leptis : two pillars in the west apse, and part of a pilaster with reliefs portraying legends.*

71 *The portico of the Pantheon in Rome.*

Whenever there was a sharp change in the weather which I did not like, I would go out of my apartment and walk in this portico for a while. It always had a climate of its own. It was dry when it rained, cool in the heat, sheltered from the wind, and free from the falling snow. It is a place where one can always talk tranquilly to a friend.

Classical Rome was full of them. When a rich man or an Emperor wished to flatter the citizens, one of the things he frequently did was to present them with a brand new portico. They were splendid affairs, with gleaming marble columns and statues. There were porticoes round all the Imperial Forums, there were the long porticoes which led through the Campus Martius, and there was, above all, the great, three-sided portico that Pompey built, and in which Julius Caesar was struck down.

90

They were probably a Greek invention. A porch (*stoa*) was built in the agora at Athens (where it has been disastrously rebuilt by over-eager 'restorers'), where philosophers could talk and hammer out a philosophy that took its name from the place. The Stoics came to Rome and made a living by teaching in, once more, the porches. Porticoes and colonnades sprang up all over the Empire. They were so popular that when rich men built villas they felt it essential to have one to themselves. It surrounded a garden in the heart of the house on all four sides. In Pompeii, I have often walked in the porticoes, thinking, always, that no better idea for a Mediterranean dwelling had ever been thought of. The Middle Ages agreed with me. These private porticoes came back in the shape of monastery cloisters. One other man saw their charms, even in chilly England. The eighteenth-century architect, John Nash, designed two long, curving porticoes for his new Regent Street. I can, as a very little boy, still remember them. They were torn down, and now, walking down Regent Street on a cold, sleeting winter's day can be a very grim experience.

Besides their porticoes, the citizens of Leptis had another meeting place. It is located a short distance away from the theatre, its yellow walls, built of huge blocks of stone, still standing. Inside them, it looks like a cathedral without a roof. Immense columns stand against the walls with deeply-carved capitals. At one end is an apse with two columns even bigger than those in the nave. Everywhere there is rich decoration, intricate tendrils weaving about stone medallions portraying legends. It is a masterly piece of architecture, one of the finest in the whole Empire, but one's first, overwhelming impression on entering it is wonder at the vast amount of money it must have cost.

It is the Basilica, and it was a present from Septimius Severus to his home town. I have said that there is no sure evidence that he ever came back. But archaeologists who have excavated Leptis feel sure that he must have returned. If they have, as yet, no inscription to prove it, their belief has human nature on its side. It is difficult to believe that Septimius Severus, having ordered this magnificent place to be built, could have resisted the temptation to make the short sea-journey from Rome (it only took two days) for the sake of seeing it.

The Basilica was the Court of Law of the city. The apse was for the judge. When it was new, the Basilica had an upper gallery. This was for the public, who could also crowd the great nave to listen. We have no record of the procedure there, but we have ample evidence of what went on in the basilicas at Rome. There could have been little difference, for the Romans imposed their legal proceedings on all their subjects, allowing them to keep only such of their own laws as suited their Imperial convenience.

The Romans attached so much importance to *gravitas* – a dignified, self-controlled, grave manner, that it might be thought that trials were conducted with the hushed solemnity of the Supreme or the British Courts of Justice. It was quite the reverse. Trials were sometimes abandoned because of the sheer noise and confusion.

In the time of the Roman Republic, lawyers were not allowed. Cases were pleaded by prominent men, such as senators, and they were strictly forbidden to take fees. By the time of Septimius Severus (and before) such high-mindedness had been discarded. Cases were still argued by prominent people (it was an

72–74 *Remnants of the Basilica. Below left, a general view. Left, capitals of the pillars. Below, detail of one of the carved pilasters.*

75, 76 *Above, the apse; right, the massive pillars, fallen and still standing.*

essential step in a political career) but they did take fees, and, as now, they were swingeing ones.

Some knowledge of the law was essential, of course, to argue a case, but it was not the most important thing. Counsel had to have a fine voice and a gift of rhetoric. He expected, and was given, free play. The more he embroidered his theme, the better he was considered. The orators often carried this to a degree that exasperated the litigant. Martial puts it very succinctly: 'You,' he says to his counsel, 'with a mighty voice and every gesture you know, make the Court ring with Cannae and Mithridatic War, and insensate Punic perjuries and Sullas, and Mariuses and Muciuses. Now mention, Postumus, my three she-goats.'

The reason for this was that the public packed the Court and enjoyed the whole thing as a spectacle. A really good orator drew an audience like a famous

actor. If he delivered a particularly striking passage, the spectators would burst into applause. Some orators even hired *claques* to clap in the right places. In Rome, four trials were held in the Court simultaneously, but, be it noted, in separate alcoves, in the same open hall. Each had its audience, each audience applauded or shouted approval. That was not the only disturbance. We learn of one occasion when the orator had such a powerful voice that everybody at the other trials listened to him, and applauded *his* fine passages, not those of the orators at the trial they were attending. The other counsel gave up.

A father, ambitious for his son, took care that his training began early, while he was still a boy. He would be sent to study under the *rhetor*, a teacher of rhetoric. Here he was set exercises. He had to declaim on set themes ('The Bull of Phalaris' was a favourite) and to treat them in a pre-established manner, according to unvarying rules. The theories were deliberately chosen to have no relevance

77 *Personification of the Roman Senate and the People, 1st century AD, from a relief found beneath the Palazzo della Cancelleria.*

78 *A Roman relief of the 4th century AD presumably representing a philosophical argument.*

to the boy's surroundings or current events. A completely empty windiness was what was aimed at, and to judge from the examples that have survived, the teachers most fearfully succeeded.

The rules of rhetoric had a curious history. The science was revived in the Renaissance. It affected the University of Bologna. Bologna set the style for all the other universities in Italy. It gave rise to a special way of speaking, very elaborate, very studied. It was called the 'aulic' style: that is, one used in the lecture hall. It bedevils trials in Rome to this day. One can still hear a fine burst of rhetoric delivered in the most mellifluous voice, and one can still hear applause from the public, who continue, a little guiltily, to love it.

The basilica, too, has survived. When Christianity became legal in the Roman Empire under Constantine, the Christians had no churches. They met in one another's houses. When they were free to build, they confronted a problem. The only places of worship in existence were the hated pagan temples. They could not be copied, and, in any case, they were not designed for the Christian ritual. The basilicas were, however, ideal. The altar was placed in front of the apse, the bishop sat where the judge had sat, and the congregation gathered in the wide space between the walls. When this grew too small, transepts were added left and right of the altar to cope with the overflow. Thus the design of a Christian church was established and lasted to modern times. The four great pilgrimage churches of Rome still bear the name of the Roman Courts of Law.

It is to this fact that we owe the preservation of the great Basilica of Leptis. When the Roman Empire became Christianized, the Basilica became a church. With capitals looted from other buildings, the Leptis Christians built a pulpit. It lies, now, in ruins. But that was the only thing they did to the building. The Basilica has come down to us otherwise untouched, the finest relic of its kind in the whole Roman world.

79 A Christian pulpit, which re-uses earlier capitals in the Severan Basilica, Leptis Magna. ⟩

< 80 *Detail of the Medusa arcade in the New Forum, Leptis Magna.*
81 *Pillars of the theatre proscenium, with* PROSCAENIUM *inscribed, Leptis Magna.*
82 *Phallic symbol from a door lintel, Leptis Magna.*

The Harbour

The harbour of Leptis Magna is scarcely a ruin. So much is left of it that it could be used again. Ships could tie up to its bollards, were there any water: goods could be loaded and unloaded on the harbour steps; and, with the aid of some roofs, the goods could be stored in the warehouses. It is as evocative as Pompeii.

It lies between two headlands, each crowned with massive ruins that jut out boldly into the sea, the waves beating and breaking against the gigantic stones of their foundations. Between them lies what was once the harbour. It is silted up now, and covered with bushes. You cross this as though you were a ship. Before you, rising as you walk, is the long quay. Stone steps run down to the water-level, so unworn and so complete they look as though they have hardly been used. Indeed, the whole quay is so fresh-looking that the archaeologists were driven to put forward a theory. They surmised that shortly after Septimius Severus had it built, the trade of Leptis suffered a sharp recession from which it never recovered.

Certainly something strange happened. The stone bollards that line the edge barely show the marks of the hawsers of the ships that were tied to them. Behind them runs a colonnade, and the columns seem fresh from the chisel. We shall probably never know the reason. Men do not put up inscriptions to record a slump in trade.

On one promontory are the foundations of a lighthouse: on the other, rise the thick walls of a tower that was used to control the comings and goings of the ships. Behind this are the remains of a temple to Jupiter Dolichenus, with a magnificent flight of steps leading down to the harbour. There is a deep silence here, broken only by the sound of the waves far below. It is the best place in Leptis to walk and dream. But to business, like the Phoenicians.

83 *Ruins of the lighthouse in the harbour of Leptis Magna.*

84 *The harbour of Leptis Magna.*

The merchants of Leptis Magna no longer depended on barter with savages. The trade which left their great port and which made them rich was with Rome, the seat of the masters of the known world. Rome was the centre of their thoughts, the subject of their conversations, the source of their hopes and fears. It was to Rome that they went to make their bargains, sailing in their famous ships to Brindisi or Naples, jolting up the Appian Way in four-wheeled carriages or swaying litters. It was in Rome that they picked up the news and the gossip they would retail back in Leptis. To understand them, we must follow them.

When the port that we see today at Leptis was built, the merchants made their money chiefly from two things: the export of olive oil and wheat, and of wild beasts for the amphitheatre. Romans could not live and be happy without either, and it is to these that, like the merchants of Leptis, we must turn our attention. It is in many ways an extraordinary story, which leads, step by step, to an unexpected end – the men of Leptis found themselves with one of their own sons on the throne of the Empire.

85 *Mooring rings in the harbour.*

We all learned at school that the Emperors kept the people of Rome content with 'bread and circuses'. The 'bread', with which went olive oil, was a dole. First, let us see what the dole really was.

Since I have known Rome, it has quadrupled its population. As soon as the Second World War was over, Italians from all over the peninsula flocked to Rome, attracted by the glamour of its name. Ancient Rome had a similar problem. It began as a small city, but with the rapid growth of its Empire, it expanded. Scholars will never cease arguing about how many people lived in it in Imperial days, but the best guess is that it was over a million, a gigantic mob for those days when there were far less people in the world.

Rome's chief job was administration. The whole Empire was run from the palace on the Palatine hill. This was done largely by bribery and corruption, which meant that any ambitious man, from any part of the world under Roman rule, must come to Rome to keep an eye on his affairs. Even men who were ambitious for nothing but living a quiet life in the country on their estates, found

86 *Hunting wild beast, mosaic from Djemila (Algeria), late 4th or early 5th century.*

it wise to have a house in Rome to carry favour with the Emperor and thus be sure of retaining their heads and their property.

All these, too, had to eat, dress, and build, but there was an army of slaves to look after them. This meant that for a great number of the immigrants, there was nothing to do, and no way of earning steady money. The Emperors solved the problem in a thoroughly modern way. They taxed the Empire without mercy and gave the money away to the citizens. This form of social security was concealed by making the donations on occasions for rejoicing – a victory, the birth of a son, and so forth. They backed this up by making sure that the permanently unemployed had at least something to eat. Permits were issued to enable them to have free bread and oil.

But it should be noted that this applied to only a part of the population. At its peak, the dole catered for no more than 300,000 people. Enough, however, to keep Leptis rich.

Wild Beasts

A parallel with our own times which I have given can help us, in a very rough way, to understand the free distribution of bread (in the form of measures of corn) and oil. When it comes to the circuses, we are completely at sea. We can perhaps have sympathy with the quarter of a million Romans who regularly packed the Circus Maximus to watch the chariot-racing: that fifty thousand as regularly went to the Colosseum to watch gladiators slaughter one another, or cheer mock naval battles which were imitations in all respects save that the participants were actually killed, we must confess that we do not understand. But perhaps we should not be too proud of our more delicate natures. We have never seen gladiatorial fights. If we had the chance given to us by some future tyrant, would our sensitive spirits last? We have the story of Alypius to warn us. He was a pupil of St Augustine in Carthage. He was very much addicted to horse-racing, but St Augustine cured him of that. Then he came to Rome. Fortified by the great saint's teaching, he firmly refused to go to the public spectacles. That was a difficult attitude for a young man to maintain in Rome. One day his companions took him by main force to see the gladiators fight. He went, but kept his eyes closed. Hearing a great roar of applause, out of sheer human curiosity, he opened them. From that moment on, he had a greater passion for the gladiators than he had for the horses.

Fortunately, the good merchants of Leptis did not supply Rome with gladiators, so they need not concern us. But they did do a brisk trade in wild beasts, caught in the African hinterland by hunters, caged and shipped from the great harbour of Leptis and other Punic towns along the coast, and sold at high prices to eager buyers in the capital.

◁ 87 *Exterior of the Colosseum (Flavian Amphitheatre) in Rome.*

The Romans had a vivid interest in wild animals, the more exotic the better. They were fond of elephants, whom they thought sagacious. They marvelled at giraffes: they made pets of jaguars and leopards (the Emperor Elagabalus used to invite them to sit at his table among his guests). In a way, these beasts were a mark of Empire, like the Indian princes who were paraded at Queen Victoria's jubilees. Travel was difficult, slow and expensive. It was only for the rich. To the ordinary man in the Forum, the Empire could be no more than a series of tales: these strange animals were proof that he really ruled the world. It is even recorded that the Romans were shown a Polar bear. Since this must have been brought from the Arctic wastes of Russia, it demonstrated, unmistakably, that Rome had the money and power to have anything it wanted.

They also liked to see animals killed. Man is a hunter, and there is nothing to be done about it; but only the Romans turned the hunting of animals into a spectator sport. The Colosseum was tastefully decorated with trees and bushes so that it resembled a forest. Hundreds of wild animals were then let out of dark dungeons underneath into the full glare of the Roman sun. Huntsmen then shot them down, to the huge enjoyment of fifty thousand spectators who did not lift a finger except to clap their hands. Sometimes the Emperor would arise in his royal box, take a bow or a javelin, and despatch a few himself, carefully protected by barriers, nets, and huntsmen ready to despatch any animal that was so lacking in respect as to try a leap at the master of the world.

Not all the Emperors were marksmen, but all gave wild beast shows to please their subjects. Augustus Caesar was a pacific man who wore long flannel underpants and liked playing simple games with cheerful little boys. He gave twenty-six wild animal displays: 3,500 animals were killed. This was before the Colosseum was built, so things were on a modest scale. Titus dedicated the great structure with one hundred days of spectacle. Nine thousand animals died. There was better to come. Standing to this day in Rome is a sculptured column on which is portrayed Trajan's victory over the Dacians. But the Romans needed something more exciting than bas-reliefs. He gave 123 days of shows. Eleven thousand animals died.

All this was very good for business in Leptis: wild animals were consumer goods that had constantly to be replaced. There were variants of the mass

88 *Hunting leopards, detail of a wall painting in the hunting baths of Leptis Magna.*

slaughter. Expert men were hired to fight particularly ferocious animals, armed with daggers or javelins. Some of these men became quite famous, and the merchants of Leptis paid tribute to them. A wall-painting has been unearthed there. It shows ten of these heroes, four of them being sufficiently celebrated to have their names written beside them. They are fighting six leopards and, with sporting impartiality, three of these beasts are named: Rapidus, Fulgentius, and Gabatius. One wonders what brought them this honour: one hopes it was because in previous combats they had always brought down their man. In this fresco, at least, two hunters are at the end of their tether, and one, Victor, is about to yield. The leopard Rapidus, I am sorry to say, is not going to survive the fight. He is about to be killed.

89, 90 The Roman gladiator. Above,
an example of a gladiatorial helmet.
Right, bronze statuette showing the
gladiator with his accoutrements.

I have remarked that I like reading Martial. He has a vivid description of one animal entertainment which was studiously designed to glut the most avid sadist among the spectators. A condemned criminal was led out to a cross in the middle of the arena, and there he was crucified. This was done in the prescribed manner, with nails through his hands and feet. As he writhed in agony, a famished bear was let loose. Smelling the blood, he attacked the crucified man. With his claws he tore the man's limbs, and then attacked the body. This he reduced to a bloody pulp, not recognizable as human at all. But, says Martial, it still writhed.

This entertainment had very little artistry. Others were designed with much more taste. Nero had a considerable sense of the theatre, as we know from the performances he gave as a singer. He astonished his subjects by actually descending from the Imperial box, armed only with a club, and boldly facing a lion. He killed it. The lion had, of course, been drugged, but it all made a pretty picture.

Even prettier was the show put on to illustrate the legend of Orpheus. It tells how he charmed wild beasts with his playing on the lyre, till the lion lay down with the lamb. Later, however, the beasts tore him to pieces. Some unfortunate was chosen to play the part of Orpheus. He was suitably dressed, and given a lyre. He played on this, striking, no doubt, a number of false notes. He soothed animals that had already been stupefied. Then came the end of the story. A horde of famished beasts were released into the arena. They tore him limb from limb.

91–95 *Above, Orpheus and the wild beasts, detail of a pavement mosaic at Leptis Magna.*
Below, fight between an elephant and a bull, copy of a mosaic from the Aventine, Rome.
Opposite, three representations of gladiatorial combat in mosaics from the Torre Nuova, Rome.

Commodus

The Roman passion for the amphitheatre not only put money in the pockets of the citizens of Leptis, it played a large part in making one of them the Emperor. Septimius Severus was born in Leptis in AD 146. He was the son of a successful and distinguished family; two great-uncles of the boy had risen to the honour of being Consuls. On his father's side he had mixed Libyan and Punic blood, a fact which earned him a mention in the Senate of the United States. In July 1963, a senator arose and declared that Septimius Severus was a bad Emperor because he was part Negro. He was not, of course, a Negro. But he was not Roman. He was so much a son of Leptis Magna he spoke Latin with a thick Punic accent.

He was well-educated in Leptis and then sent to Rome to have some metro-politan polish put on him, and to make his career. The Emperor was Marcus Aurelius. He took Severus under his wing and steadily promoted this boy from Leptis, so I must spare a word for him.

Marcus Aurelius Antoninus is quite the best known of the good Emperors, and he is often portrayed as too good to be true. He owes this largely to a piece of luck. He was a man with a taste for philosophy and quiet. Unfortunately, barbarians had begun that pressure on the Roman Empire, which, in the end, was to destroy it. For this reason he had to spend most of his life in camp, waging wars he thoroughly disliked. To console himself, he kept a notebook of such profound thoughts as came his way in the middle of the military hurly-burly. The book, now known as his *Meditations*, very nearly went the way of thousands of other books. Only one copy survived the disasters of the fall of the Empire, and the Middle Ages. That, too, is now lost, but in AD 1555 it was printed at Zürich and immediately became popular.

⟨ *96 Marble bust of Commodus as Hercules, c. AD 190.*

97 *Marble head of Septimius Severus from the Temple of the Severi, Djemila (Algeria).*

A great part of the book is taken up with an explanation of the Stoic philosophy, and is somewhat stodgy. He was, however, a man who thought a good deal about himself, and he weaves into the philosophy a self-portrait. He draws himself as a dutiful son, a respectful pupil, an Emperor who held the good of his subjects close to his heart, with more than one hint that he did very well by them. He also gives endless sage advice about taking things as they come, keeping one's temper, and so on. These things alone would not have made the book as popular as it has always been. What gives the book its undeniable charm is that, as we read it, we see that a middle-aged Roman Emperor can have the middle-aged thoughts of the most ordinary middle-aged man, and that is rather reassuring. He says, for instance, 'the man who reaches the age of forty and has any sort of wits about him has seen all that has been, and will be, because all things are the same.' He disguises it with a philosophical argument, but it is the thought of millions of men as they put on their slippers in the evening.

98 *Head of the elderly Marcus Aurelius, c. AD 175.*

Marcus Aurelius would have led a blameless life – he was convinced he did – if it had not been for one thing. Like many people with an itch to talk profoundly about human nature, he was a very poor judge of it in practice. His wife's morals were the scandal of Roman society, and we can be certain that important people did not fail to let the Emperor know it. He, on the other hand, was convinced that she was chaste and faithful, and nothing in the world would make him change his opinion. When she died, the sorrowing widower asked the Senate to declare her a goddess. The Senate dutifully obliged.

It was the custom for Emperors to choose their successor, so that he could gain some experience of ruling the world. Mostly they chose someone whom they considered able, and adopted him as their son. Marcus Aurelius chose his own son, Commodus, to succeed him. Commodus set himself to be the worst Emperor that it is possible to conceive. The best that can be said of him is that he thoroughly enjoyed doing it.

Meantime, Septimius Severus continued his steady rise. In AD 190 he became Consul, and later, the Governor of Pannonia. There was only one place higher for him to go, and that was the emperorship. He set his sights on it, as well he might, for Commodus behaved in a manner which made it plain that sooner or later, a new Emperor would be called for.

There is an excellent bust of Commodus in the Capitoline Museum. It is meant to be flattering: it shows him as a handsome, well-built man, dressed as Hercules, for he fancied that he was the re-incarnation of that god. Even so, the sculptor could not resist carving the truth. It is quite clear from the portrait that Commodus had the mental equipment of a sports-mad schoolboy.

There is some doubt about his actual boyhood. The contemporary historian Dio Cassius says that he behaved himself. Others, writing later, said that he was lewd, foul-mouthed and sadistic, even as a lad. Considering his subsequent behaviour, this seems likely, and Dio Cassius may have merely been protecting the memory of Marcus Aurelius. At any rate, the story goes that at the age of 12 his bathkeeper drew his bath too cold. Little Commodus immediately ordered him to be thrown into the bath furnace. The other attendants threw a sheepskin into it instead. The stench, presumably, satisfied the small fiend.

He celebrated his adolescence by setting up a brothel of women with whom he disported himself. This was later to grow, when he became Emperor, to a harem of three hundred women and three hundred boys, chosen expressly and solely for their bodily beauty. He himself often turned up at the amphitheatre dressed as a woman, in which costume it pleased him to occupy the Imperial box. He enjoyed the more degrading forms of sexual intercourse, a thing which shocked his subjects, but does not seem too strange to us, since we can see it as an inevitable part of his psychological make-up. Reading through some of the moralizings in his father's *Meditations*, one is inclined to see Commodus as a son in revolt against a suffocatingly good father. His contemporaries, however, saw him as a bundle of pure, wilful evil. They may have been right.

Rollicking in sex alone would not have brought him the condemnation of the Romans: throughout their history, the Romans never made up their minds about sexual freedom, until the Christians made it up for them. Their attitude

99 *Representation of a chariot race, from a Roman terracotta relief, now in the British Museum.*

can best be summed up by the story that Plutarch tells about the elder Cato, a man who liked to be thought an upholder of public morality. Seeing a lad emerge from a brothel, he said, approvingly, 'Good: good'. Passing the same brothel on another occasion, he saw the boy come out again. 'I did not', he said, 'mean every day.'

But where Commodus profoundly offended the Romans was in his mania for chariot-racing, and gladiators. Champion drivers and successful gladiators were public heroes. But they were also despised as belonging to the lowest of professions. Commodus, the son of Marcus Aurelius, and Emperor, chose to drive chariots himself. What was worse, he fought gladiators, at first in the privacy of his palace, but afterwards, in public.

He fought them with certain precautions. He was protected by two attendants who were ready to cut down any gladiator who showed signs of taking the

Emperor's sport too seriously (though Commodus, while learning the art, often cut off their noses). He also supplied his opponents with swords of lead.

Commodus might have got away with these amusements if he had continued to practise them in the privacy of his palace. But he decided to come out into public and show off his skills in the amphitheatre in full view of the public. He thus deliberately degraded the office of the Emperor. Attendance at these exhibitions was obligatory, from Senators downwards. While privately expressing its disgust, the public turned up and dutifully cheered their master.

We are fortunate in having a description of what went on from the hand of a sober historian, Dio Cassius. He apologises for describing what he does: he agrees that it might be thought that he was lowering the tone of history. But he pleads that he was there when these things happened: he saw them with his own eyes; and he frankly admits that, in fear of death, he even forced himself to show his approval. Such a man makes a very reliable guide, and from now on, I shall follow his account.

Commodus made his entry into the amphitheatres in great style. Dio Cassius reports it, and his description is worth repeating for most of us have a mental picture of a Roman Emperor being soberly dressed in a toga. Commodus wore a white silken tunic, interwoven with gold. He changed this for a purple robe with gold spangles and a crown made of gold, set with jewels from India. Since he considered himself Hercules, the symbols of that god – a lion's skin and a club – were carried before him, and solemnly given a chair to themselves in the Imperial box. He also had a fancy for being Mercury, so he himself carried Mercury's winged wand. When the time arrived for the games to begin, he did another change: he dressed in the simple dress of Mercury, a tunic and no sandals. Thus attired, the ruler of the world began his performance.

The morning was given over to killing animals. In one such exhibition, he killed one hundred bears by his own hand. He did this, admittedly, from the safety of the surrounding balustrade, but he was apparently an excellent marksman. As for the audience, Dio Cassius is very honest about them and himself. On one occasion, Commodus grew thirsty, and drained off a large container of wine at one gulp. 'At this,' says Dio, 'both the populace and we [i.e., the

Senators] all immediately shouted out the words so familiar at drinking bouts, "Long life to you".'

As a matter of record, they shouted out a number of other compliments, in a rhythmic chant, of which we have one specimen: 'Thou art Lord, and thou art first, of all men the most fortunate. Victor thou art, and victor thou shalt be: from everlasting . . . thou art victor.'

Although attendance was compulsory, many dodged it. The reason was that there was a widespread opinion that one day Commodus would start shooting at the spectators, in imitation of one of the labours of Hercules, when he shot down the Stymphalian birds. It was not, remarks the historian, beyond him. He had one day conceived the fancy of collecting together all the men of the city who had lost their feet. He had some material bound about their knees so that they looked like snakes. Then he beat them to death with a club. A few shouts were a small matter if they would ward off such a man.

He had a sense of humour, grim, as would be expected. One of his feats was to shoot arrows at the necks of ostriches, cutting off their heads. We know from other sources that it was usually done by tipping the arrow with a razor-sharp head, shaped like a sickle. On this occasion, he merely took a sword and hacked off the poor bird's head. Taking the severed head in one hand and his sword in the other, he went over to where the Senators sat. He said nothing, but wagged his head in a highly significant way, meaning he could do the same to any Senator if he wanted to.

A strange passage follows, that illuminates the state of barely suppressed hysteria in which the Senators, and others, lived under the tyranny. Dio Cassius says that he is certain that many of them would have been cut down on the spot, if they had laughed. They *wanted* to laugh, but Dio saved them. He took some laurel leaves from his garland and chewed them, making his companion Senators do the same. 'So,' he writes, 'by the steady movement of our jaws we could hide the fact that we were laughing.'

The afternoons were given over to Commodus playing the gladiator. His favourite contest was that well-known one in which a man armed with a net and trident fights another armed with a helmet and sword. The trident was substituted by a wand, while Commodus had a wooden sword. Commodus always won. A good deal of laurel must have been chewed in the Senatorial box. It is recorded that Commodus fought as a gladiator seven hundred and thirty-four times.

It may be asked how such a man could rule the Empire. The answer is that he did not rule it at all. He left that to his favourites. The first was Perennis. He took the time-honoured course of encouraging Commodus in his vices, and thus taking over power himself. The soldiers, however, rebelled against him. There were troops stationed in Britain, and they sent a delegation to Commodus to protest. Commodus met them and asked them what they were there for. They said Perennis was plotting to make his son Emperor in Commodus' place. Another favourite, Cleander, said this was true. With no more hesitation than he had when cutting off the head of an ostrich, Commodus ordered Perennis to be killed, along with his wife, his sister, and his two sons. Cleander became the favourite in his place, and soon the master of the Empire.

By this time, Commodus was badly in need of money. He had managed the no mean feat of exhausting the Imperial treasure. Cleander set about raising money for him. Every office in the state was put up for sale, including that of the Consuls. He made twenty-four of them in one year. Another was to temper justice with mercy. A rich criminal could not only buy his pardon: as an added touch, he could have the judge who condemned him and the prosecution witnesses punished in turn, in a manner which could be of his own choosing.

Since the beginning of the Principate, treason against the Emperor was punished by death and the confiscation of all his wealth. Cleander elaborated this system so that to do anything better than the Emperor was held to be treason most foul. One man was executed for being better at hunting lions than Commodus: another because he was virtuous; a virtuous man obviously disapproved of the Emperor's way of life and so was eminently worthy of death. Again death meted out by the Emperor was just: therefore it clearly followed that anybody who mourned such an execution must be killed, too.

The treasury was replenished, and Commodus could proceed with his pleasures. They took on a more elaborate hue than a mere wallowing in women and boys. As well as being Hercules, Mercury, a charioteer and a gladiator,

Commodus took a fancy to posing as a great surgeon. He cut up men with scalpels and let them bleed to death.

The ordinary public took all this in its stride, until Cleander was so unwise as to let it touch the public's belly. He had a monopoly of the corn, which produced a famine. There was a riot at the horse races. Cleander called out the Praetorian Guards, but they were overwhelmed. Next he called out the foot-guards who joined the rioters. These formed a procession to the Palace, threaten-ing a general massacre of all the Emperor's supporters and menacing Commodus himself. By a curious Palace rule, to bring the Emperor bad news put the bearer in danger of instant death. Commodus was, as usual, enjoying himself, and no one, at first, dared to disturb him. At length, his sister and his first concubine bearded the lion in his den of pleasure. The crowd was demanding the head of Cleander. Commodus tore himself away from his amusements long enough to order that Cleander's head should be chopped off and thrown out of the window to the mob. The mob went home: Commodus resumed his sports, having thus acquired, with the greatest simplicity, the huge fortune that Cleander had amassed.

Didius Julianus

The Colosseum was not so called because it was big. It got its name from a colossal statue that stood beside it. Commodus had the head of this statue cut off and his own portrait put in its stead. On the base, he had an inscription carved which said that he was, in the first place, the god Hercules, and in the second 'the champion of the secutores [the opponent, that is, of the gladiator with the net and trident] and the only left-handed fighter to conquer twelve times one thousand men.'

It was naturally quite clear that Commodus was now mad. His passion for the amphitheatre had become a mental disease. Those close to him came to the conclusion (as do most people dealing with insanity at some point) that it was no good smiling at his foibles, or hoping they would go away. He was, after all, no longer a boy. He was thirty-one. He conceived a plan to murder both Consuls, and to emerge from the gladiators' cells proclaiming himself both Consul *and* secutor. This went beyond all bounds, since it trampled on what little was left of the ancient dignity of Rome. A conspiracy was formed to do away with him. An attempt was made to poison him, but his physical condition was so good that he threw the poison up. His actual end was more appropriate. An athlete called Narcissus was sent to him, and strangled him while he was taking a bath. He had reigned twelve years, nine months and fourteen days, and that was his tragedy. Had he not been Emperor, he would no doubt have been a first-class sportsman.

The choice of a new Emperor was theoretically in the hands of the Senate. In practice, it was in the hands of the armed forces, the Senators limiting themselves

to making adulatory addresses to the new man and debating with high serious-ness whether his predecessor, on dying, had become a god.

On the death of Commodus, the most likely candidate was an old man called Pertinax, whose upright life and services to the state made him the reverse of everything that Commodus had been. He proceeded, as was proper, to bribe the Praetorian Guard. This was an élite body of soldiery that had been founded by the first of the line of despots, Augustus. Augustus had picked them to look after his personal safety, and gave them double pay. There were, at first, nine to ten thousand men, but the Emperor Vitellius had increased them to nineteen thousand men, a formidable force that could easily take over Rome if they chose.

On the election of each new Emperor, it was the custom to give a donation, a gift of money, to each Praetorian. The new man usually took care that this was sufficiently large to stop grumbling. He could do this because, once secure in his position, he had the vast resources of the Imperial treasury to dip into. Pertinax, however, was in a difficult position. He was not overly rich himself. As for the Imperial treasury, he found that Commodus had left behind him only a million sesterces.* All the same, he promised to give each man 20,000 sesterces, hoping to balance the accounts by good management in the future. The Praetorians were the only people in Rome who regretted Commodus was dead: he was a man after a soldier's heart. They thought Pertinax was dull and stingy, but they accepted the bribe, at least for the time being.

Pertinax industriously set about reforms. He treated the Senate with exag-gerated respect. He promised he would put none of them to death. He avoided the mistake of Marcus Aurelius by refusing to let the Senate give his son the honorific title of Caesar. Moreover, he would not even allow him to be brought up in the palace.

*It is generally a futile exercise to try to estimate the equivalent of Roman coinage in terms of that of today. Like our own money, it was constantly being devalued. This was so particularly in the times with which I am dealing. But there is one useful indication. An African citizen left 1,300,000 sesterces in his will to charity. With the interest on this capital, at 5 per cent, he instructed that 300 girls and 200 boys of needy parents should be maintained. It will therefore be seen that 65,000 sesterces was a substantial sum of money. The donation of 20,000 sesterces to *each* Praetorian Guard can be compared with it, and judged.

⟨ 101 *Praetorian Guards, from a relief of the Hadrianic period.*

102 *Overleaf, model of the city of Rome in the time of Constantine I (AD 306–337), by I. Gismondi.*

103 *Portrait of the Emperor Pertinax (January-March AD 193), on a bronze sestertius.*

All this, as the people noted, was excellent, but he still had no money. He resorted to auctioning off the paraphernalia of sport and luxury that Commodus had accumulated. This was thrifty, but it was not very reassuring to the soldiers, who were anxious to be paid. Pertinax managed to give them 12,000 sesterces each (he claimed he gave them more) but the Praetorian Guard was a dangerous body to bilk. Pertinax, in the flurry of his reforming zeal, had strictly enjoined the Guard to be honest, and he took away their privilege of occasional looting. The Praetorian Prefect, Laetus, intrigued with them against Pertinax. To inflame the Guards, he executed a few of them, excusing himself by saying he was only obeying Pertinax's orders. It will be seen that he was a thorough man.

The Praetorians were infuriated. Two hundred of them marched to the palace and broke in upon Pertinax. He met them calmly. He made no attempt to defend himself. Faced with this noble bearing, the soldiers sheathed their swords: all save one of them. Saying 'The Guard sends you this,' he raised his sword and stabbed the Emperor. At this, all the others stabbed him, too. They cut off his head, stuck it on a spear, and carried it back to the Praetorian camp, rejoicing. About what, it is not clear. Pertinax could not have done much harm to anybody. He had ruled only eighty-seven days.

There now took place one of the most extraordinary scenes in Roman history. Didius Julianus was an extremely rich and exceptionally vulgar man. He was a Senator and a spendthrift, being particularly fond of expensive eating. He was not only greedy for food, he craved money to pay for his tastes. He was a restless man who enjoyed fishing in troubled waters: with the assassination of Pertinax, he saw a golden chance. He immediately went to the Praetorian camp. The doors were not opened to him, but he stood outside the walls, shouting. He named the donation he would be willing to pay if the Guards declared him Emperor.

But inside was Suplicianus, whom Pertinax had sent before his death to find out what was going on. He started bidding, too. Guards ran out to Didius Julianus to tell him how much. Didius Julianus raised the bid. The Guards ran back. Suplicianus did likewise. Julianus replied in kind. The bidding for the Roman Empire got so hot that Julianus was waving his fingers to indicate his offer. Finally, he raised the size of the bid so high that Suplicianus hesitated to follow him. Didius Julianus bid 20,000 sesterces per man, and the Imperial diadem was knocked down to him.

His first thought was to have something to eat. He went to the palace surrounded by his friends, towing along with him his favourite mime, Pylades. A meal was ready, but it had been ordered by the dead Pertinax, whose corpse was still on the premises. Julianus made vast fun of the menu – he always laughed and joked a great deal – and sent out all over the city to gather food and wines of the most expensive kind. He then sat down to gorge himself. While he did so, couriers sped out to the corners of the Empire with the news that Pertinax had been killed. One of them reached the Governor of Pannonia, Septimius Severus, the boy who had come to Rome from Leptis Magna.

Julianus spent his first night as the ruler of the world in playing dice. In the morning he received the Senate, including Dio Cassius. All the senators who had supported Pertinax went in fear of having their heads cut off, or at least losing their property. Dio says they moulded their faces, 'posturing, so that our grief should not be detected'. They must have provided Julianus with as much entertainment as the mime Pylades.

The common people of Rome were not so adept at acting as their social betters. They had cheerfully put up with the grotesqueries of Commodus, until his government grew so bad that they protested, not, be it marked, against him, but against his henchmen. But they took a dislike to Julianus at first sight. When he went to make a ritual sacrifice before the entrance to the Senate House, they surrounded him and began shouting. They said he had stolen the Empire, a crime of which he was quite innocent, since he had bought it. Julianus, with the customary good humour, offered them money to go away. The crowd rose to magnificent heights of moral indignation. They bawled at him that they did not want his money. Julianus, faced with their puzzling reaction – for if he could buy an Empire, it was illogical that he could not buy a crowd – lost his good humour. He ordered some of the shouters to be killed. His soldiers immediately cut them down, there, in front of the Senate House.

The crowd scattered, but gathered again in the Circus Maximus, which was directly under the windows of the Emperor's palace. There they spent the night shouting, and all the following day. They called upon the soldiers on the frontiers of the Empire to come to their aid. At last, they broke up, tired with shouting, hunger, and loss of sleep. Their cries for help were, however, answered.

Julianus, meanwhile, feasted, went to the theatre, and cracked jokes. He was servile to the Senators, not one of whom believed in the play-acting. They voted him the usual statue of gold, which he refused. He quizzically asked for one of bronze, observing that statues of gold were apt to disappear rather quickly after the death of an Emperor, whereas bronze lasted longer. He was, in a word, in great good humour again. It would appear that the biggest joke of all for him was the donative he had offered the Praetorian Guard. He did not pay it.

Now the person that the crowd had called upon to save them was Gaius Pescennius Niger, the Governor of Syria. When his troops heard of the death of Pertinax, and perhaps of the shouts in Rome, they declared him Emperor. He prepared to march on the city, but without undue haste, because he was dilatory by nature.

Septimius Severus was the reverse. He summoned his troops, harangued them about the outstanding merits of Pertinax, and urged them to avenge his murder. It is doubtful if Pertinax was really such a hero to the soldiers, but the drift of Severus' speech being clear, they, too, declared him Emperor and got ready to install him in Rome with the aid of their swords.

134

Septimius Severus had another rival besides Niger. Clodius Albinus was the Governor of Britain, an able man, but ready to make compromises. The risk of claiming the Empire was great. If he failed, it would mean certain death. Severus ingeniously played on this. He offered Clodius the title of Caesar, a share in governing the Empire, and the possibility of succeeding him when he died. Clodius accepted: Septimius Severus was free to march on Rome, his only problem now being to get to Rome before Niger.

He took his troops on forced marches. He selected six hundred men as his bodyguards, marched with them in their midst, and allowed no man to take off his breastplate, day or night. He crossed the Julian Alps, took Ravenna without striking a blow, and set out for Rome.

When the news reached Rome that Severus was approaching, Julianus struck a martial attitude. He ordered ramparts to be built (Rome had no walls at that time). He summoned the fleet from Misenium, a bold stroke of tactics, since Severus was approaching by land. He ordered the Senate to declare Severus a traitor, and, with deep, dark cunning, sent ambassadors to treat with him, together with assassins to kill him. The result of all this military bustle was comic. The soldiers in Rome had done no real fighting: they found their armour very awkward. The sailors came to Rome and proved innocent of any discipline and very uncertain in handling ships. Elephants were recruited to strike terror into the Pannonian legions but did not show much promise since they continually threw their riders. The Praetorian Guard were sullen, both at not having been paid, and having to fight. Moreover, they were frightened. Severus' soldiers had a reputation for being very tough warriors.

Julianus, at this crisis, had a flash of inspiration. Catastrophe threatened, but he felt that if he could *foresee* the disaster, he would have a chance of avoiding it. So he killed a number of boys in a magic rite. The bloodied bodies demon-strated nothing except that the master of the world had lost his head.

After boys, the Vestal Virgins. Julianus conceived the idea of sending them as a deputation to Severus in an attempt to soften his heart, but this scheme was rejected by the Senate. There was nothing left now but to offer Severus a share in the Empire as joint ruler. Julianus sent this message to Severus by one of

Severus' supporters, Vetrivius Maerinus. Severus' answer was to kill the messenger.

He had more effective messengers of his own. He let it be known that, although he could not overlook the assassination of Pertinax, the Praetorians would not be punished, provided the men actually responsible for the deed were surrendered. This left Julianus without defences. The Senate rose to the occasion in its usual patriotic manner. It sentenced Julianus to death, declared Severus Emperor, and just to be certain of being on the side of the angels, made Pertinax a god.

When the soldiers came to kill him, Julianus was in the palace. It was the sixty-sixth day of his reign. Just before they struck, he asked the soldiers, 'But what have I done? Whom have I killed?' The answer is, of course, nobody. No Senators, that is; only people.

Septimius Emperor

When Septimius neared Rome, the Senate sent a delegation of one hundred Senators to welcome him, as well as to find out what sort of Emperor their new master intended to be. Septimius soon showed them. Before they could deliver any of the fine speeches they had composed, he surrounded them with his bodyguards. Then he had them searched for arms. After they had made their speeches, he humiliated them in a second and more subtle way. He dismissed them with a handsome cash present for each Senator. The episode is highly significant. Throughout his reign he was to base himself on two things – soldiers and money. It was a successful policy. The provincial from Leptis understood Rome to perfection.

Other Emperors had shown their contempt for the Senate. Septimius' next step was unique: it changed the history of the Roman Empire.

He summoned the Praetorian Guard, the body of men who had become accustomed to making and breaking Emperors. He told them to assemble outside Rome, the field in the city where martial exercises were held. He also ordered them to leave their arms and armour in their camp. Exactly as he had done with the Senators, he surrounded them with his own hardened troops. As they stood there, not knowing whether they would be cut to pieces any minute, he read them a lecture. He rebuked them for not doing their duty. Their job was to protect the Emperor, but Pertinax had been killed. If we are to believe the historians, the Praetorians, each man of whom knew perfectly well that it was they who had caused the murder, were abashed. Septimius ordered them to be stripped of their insignia, and he banished them from Rome. Hard as it is to credit, it was an emotional scene. The men who had bargained away the Empire

104 *A bronze statue of Septimius Severus, from Kythrea (Cyprus).*

wept at Septimius' stern words. There was even more emotion when Septimius took away their horses. One horse refused to leave his master. The animal doggedly followed him, till the guard drew his sword, killed his horse, and then killed himself.

This extemporary little scene must have pleased Septimius, since he well understood the Roman craving for drama. He promptly gave two magnificent theatrical presentations. Both are worth studying. They throw a vivid light on the character of his new subjects. They explain, too, why the Romans put up so placidly with the antics of Commodus. After all, he was never less than understanding.

Septimius rode to Rome in the full panoply of the cavalry, arms, armour and all. Once arrived, he dismounted, changed into civilian attire, and entered the city on foot. The citizens ate up the charade. There was cheering and chants: people held one another up to see the new hero (they had to, since he was on foot) and they applauded the soldiers who followed him. These, however, were armed to the teeth.

The show continued with Septimius presenting himself to the Senate. He deplored the way that his predecessors had freely cut down members of that august body at their will. He instructed one Senator, Julius Solon, to draw up a decree that the Emperor could not kill a Senator, for whatever reasons, without the Senate's consent. Not long afterward, he ordered Julius Solon to be murdered. Later on, he was to put twenty-five Senators to death.

The role that Septimius was playing in this first month of his reign was that of the avenger of Pertinax. This, too, had to be dramatized, and it was done in style. First, as a sort of curtain-raiser, he ordered that Pertinax's name should be mentioned at the end of all prayers. Next, a golden image of the dead Emperor was carried round the Circus on a car drawn – a fine touch of showmanship – by elephants. The crowd would be in two minds about Pertinax, but elephants were always popular. The great Julius Caesar liked to have them about him, in processions, carrying torches.

Then came Pertinax's funeral. A platform was erected in the Roman Forum. On this was a shrine, open on all sides, and held up by columns made of ivory

105, 106 *Pertinax commemoration issue, silver* denarius *issued by* Septimius Severus *from the mint of Rome. The reverse shows an eagle on a globe.*

and gold. Under this was a bier on which reclined a wax image of the dead man. A beautiful boy kept the flies off this by waving a peacock fan.

Next there was a procession of all the notables of the city, with statues of dead celebrities, soldiers, cavalry, and a golden altar covered with jewels. Septimius spoke a eulogy, the crowd (and the Senators) joining in with shouts of approval. 'But', says the historian Dio Cassius, a little slyly, 'our shouts were loudest when he concluded.' They were all anxious for action.

It was provided. The bier was removed to the Campus Martius; the citizens wept, beat their breasts, or played dirges on flutes, Septimius Severus modestly following behind all the rest. In the Campus Martius, a pyre had been erected. It was a tower, adorned with gold and with statues. On the top, touchingly, was Pertinax's favourite chariot. The bier was placed inside. Severus reverently kissed the wax effigy goodbye. Then all took their seats on wooden stands to watch a military tattoo. It took place round the pyre, consisting in complicated cavalry rides, and displays of warfare tactics by the infantry. At last the Consuls set light to the pyre. For the finale, an eagle, no doubt terrified out of its wits by the smoke and flame, flew from out of the top of the structure, symbolizing Pertinax's soul becoming immortal.

It was all as much fun for the Romans as Commodus, but much more dignified.

The mummery over, Septimius got down to the business of ruling in his own way. The man from Leptis destroyed, at a blow, one of the Romans' most cherished privileges. By doing this, he won himself a place in history – as the man who began the decline and fall of the Empire.

Until his reign, the Praetorian Guard had always been recruited from among Romans, or from provinces that they had thoroughly Romanized – Spain, Macedonia and Noricum (a Roman province in the Alps). Septimius abolished this distinction. He made the Praetorian Guard open to any good soldier, even if he were an utter barbarian: and barbarians often made excellent fighters. He made it a reward for distinguished service on the field. He increased the pay, he allowed the new Guards to wear gold rings, and even to live with their wives. He quadrupled their number. With this band of dedicated military, he meant to rule. They vowed allegiance to him, not to Rome. They were the élite of the army, but they were not Roman in their ways, their thinking or their loyalties. If the Emperor spoke Latin with a provincial accent, some of the new Praetorians could not make themselves understood in the streets of Rome at all.

They dismayed the citizens with their uncouth manners, their harsh speech, their refusal to do in Rome as the Romans did. Septimius, at a stroke, had reduced the masters of the earth to the level of the races they had conquered. Septimius' son was to carry out his father's intentions to their logical conclusion. The once proud privilege of being a Roman citizen was extended to every free man in the Empire.

Septimius had thus pulled up one beloved tradition by the roots. He pulled up another. In the days of the Roman Republic, before Augustus, the Senate had been revered. Under the first Emperors, its members became servile, partly through fears for the safety of their skins, but partly, also, because they found that an Emperor kept them from tearing the state apart with factions. The Emperors kept the peace: wars were far-off affairs on the frontiers; there was no fighting in the streets. There was a price to be paid: every so often one of them would have to open his veins in the bath, or fall upon his sword, or bare his neck to a soldier's sword, on the Emperor's orders. But there were rewards, too. The Emperor could make one of them the governor of a province and turn a blind eye when he systematically plundered it and put the proceeds in his pocket. The Emperors were tyrants: but tyrannies, then and now, only survive because some men are making a great deal of money out of them.

The Senate, in fact, had no more power to govern than the British Monarchy of today. But just as the British monarch maintains the fiction that he or she appoints the Prime Minister, so the Emperors kept up the pretence that the Senate ruled Rome as it had done in the sturdy, independent days of the Republic. They addressed it with respect. They consulted it about things they had already made up their minds to do. They humbly observed the law that only the Senators could make them Emperors, even if it meant surrounding the Senate House with armed troops to force them to do it.

Senate and Emperor maintained the charade because it kept alive a super-stition which was fundamental to the character of every true Roman. He believed that, because he was a Roman, he was a special person. However much he might wallow in self-indulgence, he felt that deep inside him he had those virtues of discipline, steadfastness and courage that had raised Rome from being a small town beside a muddy river to being the master of all Italy, and then, of all the Western world. The feeling came in bursts. Every so often the Emperors would promulgate laws meant to return the Romans to their ancient austerity. Luxuries and display would be forbidden: laws to maintain the purity of family life would be passed: the ancient religious cults would be praised and subsidized, exotic religions, offensive to Roman traditions, would be put down. The Romans admired the regulations: they made no attempt to evade them, because it was not necessary. Nobody dreamed of obeying them.

The Senate was the unlikely symbol of all this. As we have seen, Septimius Severus was, at first, careful to follow tradition. But he was a foreigner, the first ever to be made Emperor. The Roman superstition meant nothing to him. Once he was sure of his power, surrounded by his foreign guard, he threw off his pretence. He treated the Senate with the contempt that it no doubt deserved. The Senators were reduced to a body of servile flatterers, a *claque*, ready to applaud everything he did. They never recovered their prestige.

Septimius spent a month in Rome. He was so sure of his position that, after that brief period, he rode off with his army to chase his rival, Niger. He found him, and defeated him. He cut off his head, and then proceeded to punish the towns that had been so rash as to declare for the pretender. The punishment was condign; he fined them four times as much as the money they had given to Niger.

Albinus was next. When he realized that Septimius had no intention of sharing his rule, as had been promised, he had his troops declare himself Emperor. Septimius attacked him. The battle was hard-fought. At one stage, Septimius was in danger of losing his life, but in the end he won. Albinus committed suicide. Septimius had his body thrown into the river Rhône, but his head he sent to Rome. It was displayed to the public as a warning to anybody who thought of opposing him.

Septimius ruled well, if without enthusiasm. Having won the Empire and humbled the Senate, he found that being the unchallenged master of the world was a chore. Nevertheless, he did those dull things that had been ignored for so long: he restored the public finances, he saw to it that the granaries were always full, and, most importantly, he restored dignity and fairness in the courts of justice, the rich and the poor being treated with equality. He was proud of the fact that he brought peace to the Empire, only the remote Caledonians in Britain giving him trouble. All in all, he seemed to be a man without weaknesses.

This was not so. He had the virtue of being a devoted father, and this turned out to be his worst vice, and one that in the long run turned out disastrous for the Empire.

On the death of his first wife, he set about choosing, scientifically, the best woman to be his second. Then, as now, there was a great belief in astrology. He examined the horoscopes of all the likely candidates and settled on a Syrian princess, Julia Domna. She was beautiful, she had brains, she loved talking with philosophers, she was an excellent mother. So far, it would seem that the stars had foretold correctly. She produced two sons, Aurelius Antoninus, known as Caracalla, and Geta.

With a doting father and a clever mother (both, be it noted, non-Romans), they were each educated with the greatest care, under sound and strict tutors. This they endured while they were children, but as soon as they were adolescents, they flung themselves with glee into all the pleasures that Rome had to offer two Princes Royal. Two brothers sowing their wild oats with all the money in the

world might have been forgiven: indeed, it could have been an entertaining spectacle. The trouble was that they hated each other with sibling fury. Whatever one would do, the other would strive to do better, whether it was racing chariots or seducing women and boys. The Romans took sides, just as they did at the Circus. But they were dealing with a much more serious competition, as some of them were to learn to their cost.

We do not know much about the character of Geta. That of Caracalla turned out to be so bad that his younger brother has been given the benefit of history. He is the white-headed boy who became his brother's victim. He was popular with the soldiers, which does not suggest he was a shrinking type.

As for Caracalla, he soon showed what sort of stuff he was made of. Severus had a favourite, Plautianus, whom he made Prefect of the new Praetorian Guard. Since Severus based his rule on the soldiers, Plautianus soon acquired great power and wealth. Septimius gave him office after office, even, to crown all, making him responsible for justice in the whole Empire after the hundredth milestone from Rome. It went, as usual, to the Prefect's head, but his way of showing it was at least novel. For the marriage of his daughter he had one hundred boys and men castrated so that she could be accompanied by a fitting train of eunuchs. Some of the men were of good social standing, and fathers of families. He could behave in this outrageous fashion with some safety. Septimius loved him, and admitted it. 'I love', he said, 'this man so much I wish I could die before him.'

Plautianus arranged for his daughter to marry Caracalla, a union which should have secured his power. But the marriage was not a success. This is a common occurrence, but Caracalla was no common man. He blamed the whole thing on his father-in-law and determined to make him pay for it. He told his father that Plautianus was plotting to usurp him. Severus called the man he loved so much unto his presence. Caracalla was there. Plautianus had barely time to deny the accusation, when Caracalla rushed upon him with drawn dagger and tried to despatch him with his own hands. Septimius restrained him: he ordered the deed to be done by a soldier.

The rivalry between the ferocious young man and his brother (whom the soldiers preferred) was now splitting Rome into two halves. Septimius dealt out honours to both his sons with an even hand. He went so far as to declare both of

108 *Bronze* sestertius *of the Emperor Geta (AD 211–12).*

them equal to himself. Thus, in theory at least, Rome was ruled by three Emperors. Yet this was the act of a man who throughout his life blamed Marcus Aurelius for being so fatuous a father as to make his son Commodus his heir.

Septimius decided that a spell of warfare would harden his two sons and bring them, perhaps, together in the comradeship of arms. The Caledonians were giving trouble in the north of Britain, so he set out to subdue them. He was now in his sixties, an old man racked with pain from gout, which was so bad that he often could not walk. He was carried northwards across Europe in a litter.

Caracalla grew impatient. He had the titles of power – he was, in name, an Emperor. The one thing that stood between him and the reality was his father. He made up his mind to kill him. One day, in spite of his gout, Septimius mounted a horse. His son Caracalla rode behind him. At one point, Caracalla drew his dagger and struck at his father's back. The blow was seen in time, and an aide diverted it. Septimius rose to the occasion, whether as an imperturbable Emperor or as a foolish father, it is hard to say. He summoned Caracalla to him, as he stood surrounded by his court. Caracalla's weapon lay on the ground in front of Septimius. Septimius invited him to pick it up and kill him on the spot, or, if he did not wish to do it himself, then to ask one of the bystanders to kill him.

146

It was not necessary, for he died soon afterwards, still in Britain. Before he expired he called both his sons to him. He begged them to live in harmony, a common enough thing for a dying father to say. But his next advice has rung down the centuries, for its blunt, disillusioned practicality. 'Enrich the soldiers,' he said, 'scorn everybody else.'

Geta and Caracalla were formally declared joint Emperors. If the soldiers showed a preference for the first, it was counterbalanced by the fact that Caracalla was the elder brother; moreover, Septimius had been quite clear – they were to have equal power. Thus he left behind him an Empire ruled by two brothers with murderous hatred in their hearts. It was only a question of who would kill whom first.

They returned to Rome with their father's body. Each was closely surrounded by his own guard. On the way they never ate at the same table and never slept under the same roof. Their father's funeral over, they divided the Imperial palace into two halves. Doors were sealed up and corridors closed. No intercourse between the two halves was permitted.

It was a situation which could not endure. Some attempt was made to solve it. A treaty was sketched out by which Caracalla should remain in Rome and rule Europe and western Africa. Geta should set up his capital in Alexandria or Antioch and rule the eastern half. Troops should be stationed on both banks of the Bosphorus to prevent the two Emperors flying at each other in war. It was a sensible suggestion, for the division of the Empire had already begun. The eastern half was gaining more and more power. We think of the Senate as quin- tessentially Roman. In fact, it has been estimated that one-third of the Senators came from Syria and the other Eastern possessions. Perhaps because the true Romans could sense the change all about them and feared it, they rejected the scheme.

Julia Domna (also from the East) endeavoured to make peace between her two sons. She invited them both to meet her. Geta agreed, and so did Caracalla. But he concealed soldiers near her room. At a signal, they dashed out. One of them struck at Geta. Screaming, 'Mother, save me! They are killing me,' Geta ran to her. The soldiers continued to strike, wounding Julia in the hand. Geta died on her breast, covering her with his blood. Caracalla joined in the mur-

dering, or at least, he always proudly said he did. He dedicated the sword in the Temple of Serapis at Alexandria.

His brother gave Geta a splendid funeral and then began slaughtering his friends. He ordered that anybody who had ever had dealings with Geta should be killed, they and their families. The world was forbidden to mourn him. Those that did, even those who mentioned his name, were killed as well. Even Julia, to save her life and those of her attendants, had to pretend to be happy and content. Twenty-thousand people died in order that Geta should be expunged from the memories of men.

It was a great revenge, but history has had a greater, if more subtle one. Geta's name was struck out of every inscription in the Empire, and other names fixed over the gap. One of the inscriptions is on the arch that Septimius Severus had erected in the Roman Forum. Geta's name was duly removed and other bronze letters hammered into the marble. The arch survives to this day: but the letters fell out, leaving the holes of Geta's name clearly visible. Guides never fail to point it out.

Caracalla

He was called 'Caracalla' because of a cloak he affected. I cannot say if this nickname reminded the Romans that Caligula was called after a little boot he wore as a boy, but it should have done. Both men were affected by the same homicidal paranoia.

In spite of the fact that his father had left the Imperial treasury full, Caracalla was soon in need of money, partly because of his own expenditures, partly because of his lavish donatives, and lastly because of such huge undertakings as baths in Rome, which, begun by his father, still bear his name.

He made his own attitude towards the matter clear. 'I do not wish', he said, 'anybody to have any money but myself. And I want to give it to the soldiers.' It is a phrase worth studying, for it shows how Severus' wise, if cynical, advice emerges as a piece of madness after it had passed through his son's brain.

It had been the custom of Emperors to raise money by seizing the fortunes of men who were suspected of disloyalty: Caracalla gave this practice an added depth. He made it include those who had no treasonable designs at all. He singled out those who asked no favours of him and drew them in the net. 'It is clear', he would say to them, 'that if you make me no requests, you do not trust me; if you do not trust me, you suspect me: if you suspect me, you fear me: if you fear me, you hate me.' It is the sort of logic that delighted Lewis Carroll, and the conclusion was always Carrollian, 'Off with his head.'

He did not stay long in Rome. He set out to tour the provinces, especially those of the East, where the pickings were abundant. But he did not always ruin wealthy men to put the money in his own pocket: he ruined them for the sheer pleasure of seeing them bankrupt. He would order in advance that lavish

    110 *Marble bust of Caracalla, c. AD 211.*⟩

houses be built to hold him and his court. The trembling subject would hasten to obey, spending vast sums of money in order to be sure that the Emperor would not think him mean. When the house was ready, Caracalla would refuse to live in it: sometimes he even refused so much as to give it a glance.

Another device was to order immense public works to be undertaken. This gave him great popularity with the poorer of his subjects. He would then order some rich Senator to pay the bill. All this, however, was in the way of sport: the proscriptions, the executions, and the confiscating of money for Caracalla's own use went on simultaneously. The soldiers had to be kept happy.

He had a deep admiration for Alexander the Great, and liked to be told he resembled him. To help this along, he is reported to have had a medal struck showing his own face on one side, and his face remodelled to look like Alexander's on the other. It was typical of his mental disease that while he could imagine himself as the Macedonian king, he also liked to be one of the commonest, humblest soldiers. He dressed like them: he worked beside them at their meanest tasks, and thoroughly enjoyed it. This caused considerable mirth in the city of Alexandria, where the Macedonian lay in his crystal tomb, sealed up by Septimius Severus so that no one after him should look upon the celebrated features. The Alexandrians had a noted gift for witty remarks, and they gave play to it.

This was most unwise. Caracalla had a profound sense of guilt. He constantly dreamed that his father and his brother were chasing him with swords. He would awake from this nightmare in a state of frenzy which, from time to time, drove him from paranoia to outright insanity. The Alexandrians suffered for their wit.

He descended on the city with his soldiers. He took up residence in the Temple of Serapis, the principal shrine in the city, where the sword which he claimed he had thrust into Geta lay dedicated before the altar. He then ordered a general massacre. The inhabitants were told to stay in their houses, while his soldiers occupied the streets and the rooftops. Then the slaughter began, with Caracalla going round watching the spectacle. He allowed no distinction of persons. Anybody and everybody was cut down, their bodies being thrown into deep trenches, and the bodies set on fire. Some victims were burned while still alive. Caracalla wrote proudly of all this to the Senate, adding that he did not know how many had died, but it did not matter, since all the Alexandrians had been guilty.

He concluded his punishment with an ingenious touch. He was determined that the Alexandrians, so free with their humour, should live in gloom and misery. He banned all shows and entertainments, of which the Alexandrians were inordinately fond. They were also a very social people. He therefore built a wall right across the city, well guarded, so that, as in Berlin today, the inhabitants on both sides could no longer visit one another. Thus friends were parted and families broken up. Fortunately, it was not for very long.

When Caracalla was in Syria, a fortune-teller made the rash prediction that the Praetorian Prefect, Macrinus, would one day be Emperor. The man was immediately sent in chains to Rome. He was questioned by the Prefect of the city, who discovered that the seer meant that Macrinus would succeed Caracalla. The Prefect wrote accordingly to his Emperor. Word was smuggled to Macrinus, warning him of trouble. The subsequent events throw a bright light on the casual way the Empire was governed. The Imperial dispatches were given to Caracalla. But as he was watching a chariot-race at the time, he handed them to Macrinus. The Praetorian Prefect read the news. Foreseeing his own immediate death, he decided to strike first. He employed a discontented soldier, called Martialis, to kill the Emperor.

The occasion was a journey to a famous shrine. Caracalla got down from his conveyance to answer a call of nature. Martialis, feigning some urgent message, went up to him and stabbed him to death. Martialis was instantly shot through with an arrow from one of the guards.

The Praetorian Guards, now convinced it was their solemn duty to select the Emperor, debated for a while among the possible candidates. Macrinus was so struck by grief at the death of his master that nobody suspected him of having caused it. He was elected Emperor because, as always, his was the most satisfactory bribe.

Elagabalus

Macrinus was the first Emperor who was not a Senator. This makes it difficult to say what he was really like, because we cannot see him clearly through the open snobbery of the classical historians. These were all gentlemen – or claimed to be. The more the Senate declined in power, the more each Senator was attached to his social rank, a common phenomenon in a declining aristocracy. Macrinus seems to have been indecisive: he was a poor general: and he was niggling. While he agreed to pay his soldiers at Caracalla's extravagant rates, he wanted new recruits to go back to the lesser pay they had under Severus. So both the paid and the underpaid got together, and, at a suitable disastrous moment in his reign (he had lost a battle), they deserted his cause. He was Emperor for only a year.

Macrinus does not really belong to the story I am telling here, which, with Macrinus out of the way, reached its fantastic and, perhaps, hilarious climax. We began in Syria. We followed the Phoenicians to North Africa, and Leptis. We followed the boy from Leptis as he rose to become Emperor, diluted the army with barbarians, married a Syrian woman, and produced Caracalla.

Julia Domna, his Syrian wife, affected to take the assassination of her second son as tragically as that of the first. She may have committed suicide, or, as seems more probable, she died of a cancer of the breast from which she had suffered for some time. Julia Domna had been a clever woman in the sense of being a dedicated bluestocking, fond of discussions with philosophers. Her sister Julia Maesa was equally clever, but in a scheming, practical way. She had two daughters, Soaemias, who had a son, and Mamaea, who also had a son. This quintet was sent to live out their days in the town of Emesa, in Syria.

⟨ 111 *Portrait head of Elagabalus (AD 218–22), obverse of an* aureus.

Emesa was a small provincial town, where, it could be thought, the little family group could do no harm. But the grandmother had a huge fortune. She also had a delicately beautiful grandson, the child of her daughter, Soaemias. At fifteen, he became the high priest of the local god. The god was identified with the sun, but in fact he was a black, conical stone. We have seen that religion was the deepest passion of the people of these parts. Elagabalus, the conical stone, was worshipped with an unbridled fervour. The boy, Bassanius, even preferred to be called by the name of the god he served, and that is the name by which he is known to history.

In spite of all the crimes of the Emperors, historians so far have reserved a special shocked disgust for Elagabalus. Since we are well into the second half of the twentieth Century, I think it is time to treat him with a little more fairness.

The boy was, so far as sexual organs were concerned, perfectly male. In one of the rites to worship his conical stone, he had himself circumcized (not, be it noted, castrated, as he might have done had he been an ecstatic devotee of Isis). On the other hand, he considered himself a woman. He dressed in women's clothes, he walked like a woman, he made up his face like a woman and he took it all very seriously. Once, when someone addressed him as 'My Lord', he took some swaying steps forward, put on an arch expression, and said, 'No, you should call me "My Lady".' This, to us, is not very shocking, but it should be added, in fairness, that when he said it, he was the ruler of the Roman Empire.

Such a boy, gorgeously robed, would obviously make a spectacular priest, especially when gyrating before an altar. He attracted crowds of bemused and fascinated Roman soldiers to his temple. This was no doubt due to the attraction that delicate and fragile youths have for rough men. But it also had a deeper cause. The Roman Legions paid mere lip-service to the official religion. They were continually searching out something more mysterious and satisfying than sacrificing pigeons to man or burning a pinch of incense to a deified dead Emperor. The equivocal rites of Isis, the shower of bull's blood that washed away the sins of the followers of Mithras, had made great headway among them. This boy added a new note of mystery: and he was a member of an Imperial family.

The boy's grandmother knew well how to draw profit from the situation. She spread the lie that Elagabalus was the son of Caracalla, and therefore the

112 *Reverse of an* aureus *of Elagabalus, showing the sacred stone of Emesa – the 'Bactyl' (represented as an eagle) – entering Rome.*

rightful, blueblooded heir to the Empire, unlike the penny-pinching upstart, Macrinus. She spread largesse among the troops with a liberal hand. Young Elagabalus, acclaimed by the troops, swayed his way into the purple at the age of seventeen.

The news reached Macrinus, who gathered his troops and went to put down the usurper. The Praetorian Guards from Rome all but routed Elagabalus' supporters. But the effeminate youth mounted a horse, seized a sword, and charged at the head of his wavering troops. Macrinus took fright and fled the battlefield. He was hunted and cut down. Rome, from then on, was to know its most improbable years.

The Romans had seen their Emperors enter Rome in the midst of opulent processions, riding, crowned with the victor's wreath, in a chariot. Elagabalus entered Rome, walking backwards. There was, indeed, a grand procession, but it was in honour of the Sun God from Emesa. There was also a chariot, but in it was nothing but the black conical stone. The boy Elagabalus, gloriously altered in his High Priest robes, held the reins of the horses, and walked in reverse so that he should not have to take his eyes off his God. Courtiers went behind him to catch the master of the world, should he fall.

He ordered two temples to be built, one on the Palatine, another on the Quirinal. He then collected all the other gods of Rome, together with their

157

113, 114 *Deification of the emperors. Left, a* consecratio sestertius *issued by Marcus Aurelius for Antoninus Pius. Below, a relief showing the apotheosis of Antoninus Pius and his wife Faustina, 2nd century AD.*

115, 116 *In the mystery religions practised by many Romans, rites were performed to Mithras (opposite above) and Isis (opposite below).*

sacred symbols, and brought them to stay in attendance upon Rome's newest deity.

Elagabalus now set out on his career as the Emperor-Empress of Rome, and he conducted it in a consistent manner. He took to himself, it is true, five wives in three years but this should not deceive us: their purpose was to give him a better insight into being a woman. He married the other way round (that is, as a wife) several times, once, at least, with great sincerity. There was a Carian slave called Hierocles; he was handsome, with a fine head of yellow hair. Once when driving a chariot in a race, he fell out of his chariot in front of the Imperial box. His helmet rolled off and Elagabalus fell head over heels in love with him. He was taken immediately to the palace where that night he acquitted himself excellently as the Empress's husband. Elagabalus took pains to make it a convincing marriage in all respects, including adultery; that is to say, Elagabalus would go to bed with other men in such a fashion that he was sure to be caught. Hierocles would be very angry and beat him. Elagabalus would then go about the palace and the city, proudly displaying a black eye.

It may be wondered why the citizens of Rome did not rise in wrath and get rid of this travesty of an Emperor. There are two reasons: the first is that he was a Syrian in all his ways. Since Septimius Severus, Eastern things had grown fashionable: Easterners increasingly filled high offices. If Syrian morals were lax, it was only to be expected. Their abominations, which so annoyed the Jews, were of a respectable antiquity. The second reason was broader. Ever since the time of Augustus, transvestites had been a common sight in the Roman Forum. They paraded on the Via Tuscus, right under the palace. Their favourite victims were open-mouthed provincials, whom they caught while the visitors were staring at the wonders. They gulled them in every sense, leaving them penniless. The Romans considered it all most disgraceful, but very amusing. I might remark that they do so today. If the innocent tourist observing a fine moon in the sky goes to see the Colosseum as his forefathers did, he will find well-dressed, chattering girls lurking about the cavernous depths. These are boys. There is another ancient monument, on the other side of the Tiber, the Castel Sant'Angelo, the remains of the tomb of Hadrian. Here, on a fine holiday evening, the transvestites will parade up and down, dressed in the height of elegance. Respectable husbands and wives drive by in their utility cars to watch the show. Like Romans in the time of Elagabalus, they think it reprehensible, but fun.

Elagabalus was, however, the ruler. He had to govern the Empire; for that he had to choose his officials and advisors. No man in power has ever found a foolproof way of choosing out wise counsellors and aides. Elagabalus had his own criterion. He chose men who had outsized penises. He had a team of investigators going round the public baths: any likely candidate would be hurried off to the palace. Many got jobs. A charioteer was made prefect of the fire-brigade, in those days an influential position. The most vital factor in the life of the capital was the corn supply. This was entrusted to a hairdresser. Whatever may be said about Elagabalus' system of selection, it was at least democratic.

He brought a feminine touch to life in the palace. He loved flowers. He had them strewn everywhere: guests sometimes waded knee-deep in them. He had little surprises for them in the way of floral decoration. The ceiling would open and a great shower of blooms would descend. One guest got buried in the heap and was stifled to death.

There were party games and charades as well. A favourite was for Elagabalus to stand at the door of his room, stark naked, and painted like a prostitute. Male friends would stroll up and down, like men looking for a street pick-up. One would be elaborately struck by the beauty of the Emperor. He would approach with a suggestion. Elagabalus would haggle over the price, a bargain would be reached, and the man invited inside. The game over, the lover would be loaded with gifts. Elagabalus was fond of such little surprises. He would sometimes give away a whole solid silver dinner service.

He was what the Victorians considered so desirable in a girl; he was accomplished. He could dance, sing, and play several musical instruments. He could cook. On the negative side he had moments of flightiness: and he could have tantrums. A low-class boy from Sumona called Aurelius Zoticus, an athlete, had the most beautiful body and enormous private parts. Inevitably, he was taken to the palace. Elagabalus was hopelessly enamoured. Aurelius seemed

117 *A marble bust of the 3rd century, believed to be a portrait of Julia Mamaea, the ambitious mother of Elagabalus.*

all set for a meteoric career in the civil service. But the Emperor's husband, Hierocles, was, as we have seen, a jealous man. He arranged for a potion to be slipped into the athlete's drink which rendered him impotent all night. Elagabalus, enraged, had the unfortunate Aurelius driven from the palace, then out of Rome, and finally, out of Italy.

Julia Maesa, his grandmother, had intrigued to make him Emperor, thinking that he would be easy to handle. Now she began to have her doubts. Her hold over him began to slip. We can surmise that she was beginning to suspect that her grandson's feminine wiles were a match for her own. They were, however, not quite a match. She turned her attention to her other grandson. He was a boy of suitably weak character, and entirely under the thumb of his mother, Mamaea. Julia suggested to Elagabalus that he would have more time to devote to his namesake, the conical stone, if he adopted his cousin as his son, and gave him some of the chores of being an emperor. Elagabalus was sincerely devoted to his duties as High Priest (he had even gone so far as to rape a Vestal Virgin in honour of the god), so he readily agreed. Mamaea was as big an intriguer as her mother.

The two women now set about persuading the soldiers that it would be more honourable to be led by a man rather than a female Commander-in-Chief. They heartily agreed. They began to turn against Elagabalus, and made much of young Alexander, a boy of thirteen.

It was not long before Elagabalus saw the danger. He made some ill-organized attempts to have Alexander done away with, which only served to anger the military. There were riots, and the soldiers threatened the Emperor with death, both him and his favourites. Elagabalus went to the Praetorian camp, fell on his knees in front of the soldiers, and burst into tears. He pointed to his throat and asked them to spare him his husband, Hierocles. If they could not do that, he begged them to kill Hierocles' wife (that is, the Emperor) then and there.

Some sort of understanding was patched up, but it did not last. Mamaea began bribing the soldiers, and spread tales about the humiliations that Elagabalus was heaping on the head of their darling, Alexander. Elagabalus, in desperation, formed another plot against Alexander's life. It was discovered. Elagabalus went again to the Praetorian camp, but realizing that the soldiers meant to kill him, he tried to escape by hiding in a box. He was found. His head was cut off, along with his mother's. Their bodies were dragged round Rome. His mother's body was lost, but that of Elagabalus was flung into the Tiber. For this reason, the Romans, ever ready with a nickname, from then on called him 'Tiberinus'. When he died, he was eighteen years old.

Alexander Severus

For three years, Rome had been ruled by an imitation woman. For the next thirteen, it was to be ruled by a real one. Alexander, who took the name of Severus, had nothing of the character of Septimius about him. He was a weak-willed boy completely dominated by his mother Julia Mamaea. It was she who ran the Roman Empire. Other women had intrigued to do so, but none had achieved actual power. Mamaea did. To conceal this a little, she flattered the Senate. She arranged for sixteen of the Senators to form an advisory committee. But they were hand-picked: and they advised what Mamaea wanted to hear.

She was aware that, after the excesses of Elagabalus, respectability would be the rule. Elagabalus' favourites were banished or put to the sword. The moral tone of the Imperial court was raised. The sexual life of the boy-emperor was governed by his mother, who was a matchmaker. A suitable girl, Sallustia Orbinna, was found for him and they were married with every propriety. But if the husband was utterly docile towards his mother, the wife, it seems, was not. Dissension grew between daughter-in-law and mother-in-law. That is familiar enough in any home, but here it took on a grimmer aspect. Sallustia's father was accused of plotting treason; both he and Sallustia were put to death.

This act seems a private burst of anger. In public matters, Mamaea was peaceable to the point of boredom. Nothing of note happened in Rome. The Praetorian Guard, finding no excuse to go Emperor-killing, turned on the citizenry for a trivial cause. The citizens took up arms. There was a three-day riot, in which the Praetorians burned down some houses. But it was settled. The Guards quarreled with the Praetorian Prefect and killed him in the customary dramatic circumstances in front of young Alexander himself.

118 Marble bust of Alexander Severus (AD 222–35).⟩

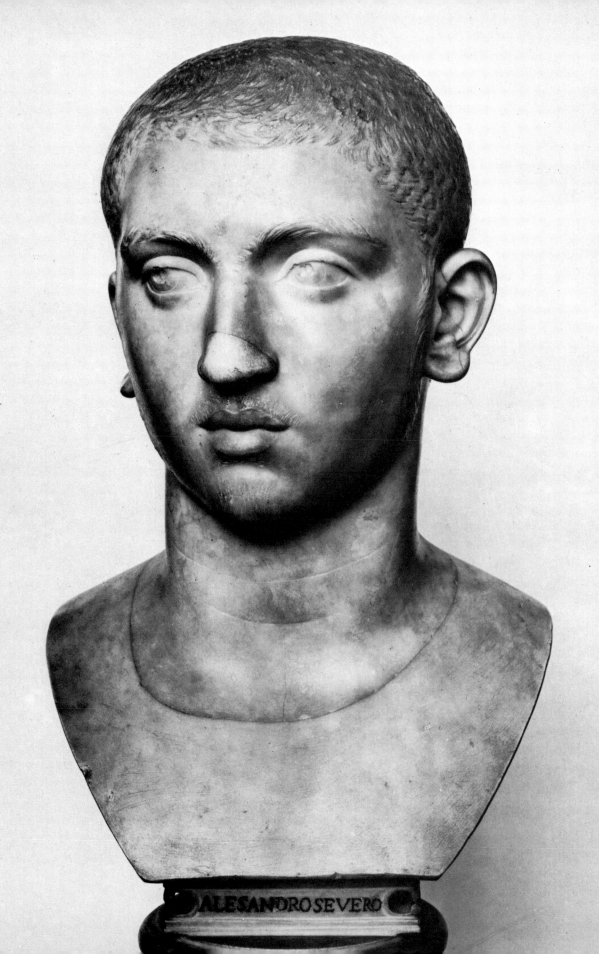

ALESANDROSEVERO

Mamaea was avaricious, a good thing for the Empire, for she would not allow her son any of the extravagances customary to an Emperor. He spent so little money that he (or rather, his mother) could reduce taxes.

So far, it might be said that Mamaea's dominance of her son did little harm. Unfortunately, it sapped his spirit. An Emperor had to lead his army, and this Alexander was far too timorous to do. Mamaea's strength lay in intrigue, not in tactics, so, inevitably, Alexander preferred negotiations to fighting. It was a disastrous policy. When Artaxerxes made himself king of the Persian Empire, he turned his arms against Rome. He rejected with contempt Alexander's offers to settle matters peacefully, forcing the reluctant boy to fight. Alexander went with his army, as custom demanded. The war began, but in the middle of it, Alexander withdrew. In the subsequent retreat, soldiers suffered bitterly. Alexander celebrated a triumph but the army began to be disillusioned.

Trouble broke out on the Rhine, with the barbarians pressing hard, destroying frontier posts, and even threatening to invade Italy itself. Once more Alexander and his mother collected an army and went with it to the centre of the trouble, at Naraz. Once more, unfortunately, Alexander preferred talking to fighting. To the disgust of his troops, he tried to buy the Germans off. The soldiers now had a very respectable reason for getting rid of him. There would also be, of course, another donative.

A man was ready. In the time when Septimius Severus was Emperor, he was one day celebrating Geta's birthday in Thrace, when a huge peasant begged to be allowed to join in the wrestling bouts which were part of the entertainment. Septimius agreed, sure that the peasant could not win against his practised soldiers. The peasant, Maximinus, took on soldier after soldier, till he had thrown no fewer than sixteen of the best wrestlers in the army. Septimius gave him a present, and enrolled him in the troops.

The next day, Septimius saw him prancing and dancing to express his joy. He acknowledged the man, at which Maximinus came up and began running beside the Emperor's horse: after a long ride, Septimius asked him if he still felt in form to do some wrestling. Maximinus said he did, and threw six opponents in succession. Septimius, delighted, took him to Rome.

There he rose in the ranks, partly because of his astounding physique, partly because he was an excellent soldier, though never losing his peasant roughness, or his peasant shrewdness.

He was at this time with the army at Mainz, in charge of training the new recruits. He was fully aware of the discontent of the soldiers with their weak little Emperor. Maximinus was the perfect contrast. He began to hint to the soldiers that he was ready to replace Alexander.

The soldiers listened. One day, when he rode out on the parade ground, they saluted Maximinus as Emperor. Alexander and Mamaea were murdered in their tent. The Severan line of rulers that started with the boy who was born in Leptis Magna thus came to an end, never to be revived.

Taxes

If we now return to the ruins of Leptis Magna: if we walk once again in Septimius' great Basilica, the elegant market place, or on the great sweep of the wharfs: if we hear voices of the past and imagine what men were talking about when these stones were whole, we shall be tempted to think that it was the news from Rome that passed from mouth to mouth – the scandals, the murders, and the fall of Emperors. This, it is true, made part of the talk. But the people of the provinces were much nearer to us than that.

I once made notes, over a year, of the topics that people spoke about, as I heard them in my own house, in the houses of others, in planes and in cars. Some spoke of their family troubles, but not all: some spoke of their egos, but not all (unless they were authors), some spoke of the news, but not always. One topic stood out from my list as the most common – taxes. It came in many forms: among the honest, laments: among the sly, hints at their cleverness in evading them: among the thoughtful, complaints about the waste of public money.

During the times I have been describing, taxes were the prime topic, if not at Rome, then certainly in the provinces of the Empire. Like us, the people found them increasingly oppressive. It is sobering to reflect that this discontent was the prelude, and largely the cause, of the collapse of the Roman Empire into anarchy.

The Emperors collected the huge sums of money they needed for themselves and the army in various ways. When a province was conquered, they imposed a tribute. This was levied on the rich landowners or public men of the territory, who passed it on to their tenants. There was also sometimes a tribute levied in kind – oil, corn and other desirable foods. Under the early Emperors, these taxes

120 *The payment of taxes, relief on a 2nd-century stele.*

were not excessive, though they were a burden. The Caesars had other resources: they taxed inheritances, they confiscated estates, they exacted excise on a wide variety of imported goods. A Roman, we read, paid over a hundred times the real price for spices and jewels from India.

But as the Emperors grew more extravagant and the soldiers more demanding, these taxes, especially those on the provinces, grew insupportable. Not only did the rich pay the tribute: any man in public office was often obliged to finance, out of his own pocket, the public works that the Emperor desired: aqueducts, roads, temples, monuments and such. They might, or might not, be able to afford it. As the burden increased, so did the number of men who dodged taking office as much as they could. One reason for the end of the Empire in the West was that, ultimately, few people could be found to run the provincial governments. It was too expensive an honour.

170

There was a worse imposition: the Emperors were constantly travelling the Empire. Wherever they went (and for as long as they stayed), the local nobility had to bear the expenses of themselves and their swarming entourage. The royal progress of a Tudor monarch through England was dreaded by their compulsory hosts, who were sometimes ruined. When the second Vatican Council decided to meet a second time in Rome during the 1960s, there was lively preoccupation in the Vatican at the cost of maintaining two thousand bishops for several months, modest as their lodgings were. It is easy to imagine what it was like to maintain a Roman Emperor.

Still, the men who had to do it were masters of immense estates, besides being gatherers of tribute, a portion of which stuck to their fingers on its way to Rome. We need not feel too sorry for them. It was otherwise with the passage of the legions.

121 *The burning of tax records, from a 2nd-century relief in the Roman Forum.*

When the Emperor sent, or led, his army off to war, they lived off the country. The people, rich, modestly off or poor, had to supply whatever they asked. They supplied the horses, the carts, the food, armour, arms, wood for the siege machines, and labour for the camps. If they were reluctant, supplies were requisitioned at the point of the sword. The soldiers also claimed the right to loot from time to time. Emperors who tried to deny them this privilege became intensely unpopular: sooner or later they were sure to be replaced, in the usual manner.

In fairness, it must be said that this whole system of taxation worked fairly well when the Empire was stable. Under such men as Trajan, Antoninus Pius and Marcus Aurelius, the Empire was prosperous. Rome sucked money into its coffers by means both fair and foul, but a good deal of it found its way back into the pockets of the provinces by that very thing with which I began this essay – trade. The sea-routes were kept open: pirates were put down (though never entirely suppressed); while the great roads, which still astonish us, bound the Empire together in a way which profited everybody. But from the time of Commodus onwards, this balance no longer held. The provincials were ruthlessly stripped; the Empire racked with war. Complaints of oppression poured in from all sides. There was only one man who could remedy them, so they poured in to the Emperor. He, however, grew steadily more and more at the mercy, not to say the whim, of the soldiery. As we have seen, they made and unmade Emperors at a vertiginous rate, demanding higher and higher rewards for doing it. In the fifty-two years between AD 235 (when Alexander Severus was killed) and AD 285, they made no less than twenty-six Roman Emperors. Of this blood-stained procession, only one died a natural death.

It was the soldiers, then, who ruled the world with a slash of their short, broad swords. It is to them that we must now turn our attention.

Timgad

For a collector of ruined cities, as I am, Timgad, at first sight, seems the perfect specimen. It lies on a sloping plain, which gives it perspective. A background of distant but not too overwhelming mountains gives it a setting which does not obtrude. There seems a lot of it left.

For an hour or two, the impression remains. It is crossed by two streets at right angles to each other. They are lined with columns, still standing in a satisfactory number. On slightly higher ground, there is the Capitol, with a temple of which two massive columns rise against the sky. Hard by is a theatre, its auditorium very well preserved. As in Leptis, there is a market place and all around it a great profusion of the lower walls of houses. At the end of the main street is a triumphal arch. There seems much to explore.

Yet, as the hours wear on, a sense of boredom begins to seep into one's spirit. The ruins seem to blend into each other, till it is hard to tell them apart. One looks for something to catch the eye and the heart, some eccentricity, some mystery, but there is little. Going down one road after another, turning endless corners, one has the feeling of being there before, not in the romantic way of a dream, but with the duller feeling of having passed that same point twenty minutes earlier. It was in Timgad for the first time in my life that I understood those people who, with little knowledge of history and untouched by the charm of archaeology, have dutifully gone around in ruins with me for the good of their cultural background, plainly longing for a glass of beer to break the monotony.

I persevered. The feeling grew with each day. It was not agreeable, but it was most instructive. I think Timgad taught me more about the Romans than Rome itself.

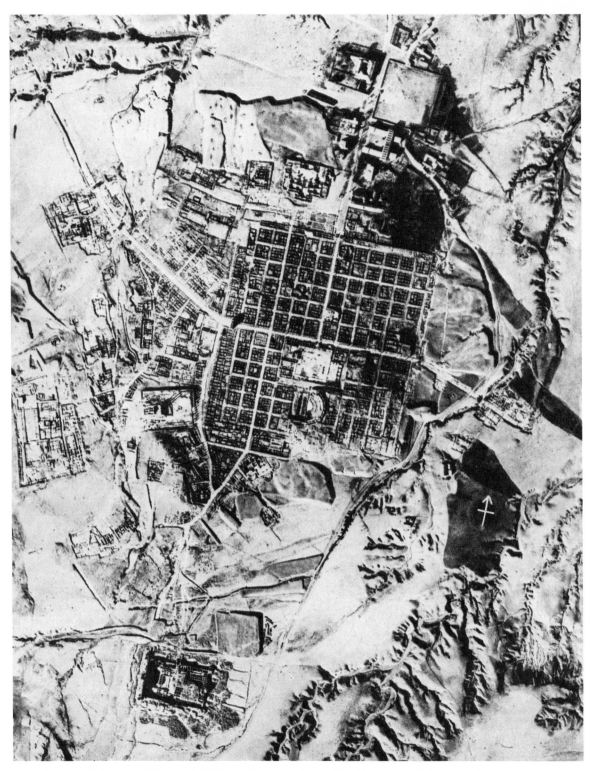

122 *This aerial view of Timgad (Algeria) shows the rigid grid system of the city plan.*

123 *A street intersection in the ruins of Timgad.*

To be properly appreciated (and to save one's feet), I think Timgad should be studied from the air. I have not done that, but I have obtained a photograph, which is on page 174, for the reader to examine.

It will be seen that it is the most formidably dull piece of town-planning that can be conceived. Even penal settlements are laid out with more variety. It is a grid of streets within a rigid square. It would do very well as a parking lot for enormous tanks. As it appears on the ground, time, earthquakes, and invaders have knocked a little variety into it. There are gaps. But when it was new, it must have looked as interesting as two rows of exactly even false teeth.

The Emperor Trajan ordered it to be built in AD 100. He was an able man who saw that it was his duty to fix the bounds of the expanding Roman Empire. He drew the lines, and protected them with forts, or with settlements which were to be inhabited by soldiers. Thus arose in North Africa, in seventeen short

175

124, 125 *Timgad: general view, and fragments of the capitol.*

177

126, 127 Opposite, a detail of the triumphal arch, which was the gateway to Timgad and, above, a view towards the arch.

years, the Colonia Marciana Traiana Thaumagas, or, as we now call it, Timgad. It lasted three hundred years, virtually unchanged, except for the erection of a very simple Christian church.

Now the Emperor Trajan was a man of taste, or at least a man who knew how to choose artists. He erected an enormous forum in the heart of Rome that was the wonder of the world. He spared no pains. He moved a whole hill to gain space for it. At one end of this imposing complex, he erected a column on which was carved a spiral of reliefs, telling vividly the story of one of his campaigns. He placed his own statue on the top, and his successors reverently put his ashes in the base. They have disappeared, but the column is still there, one of the most beautiful and satisfactory objects in all Rome.

We have seen the arch he built in Leptis Magna. It is easy to reconstruct it from the ruins that are left, and it is, as I have said, very fine. He also built an arch at Timgad. It gets by as a gateway, but without a touch of inspiration. It is a mechanical job, all nicely balanced, as the draughtsman was taught. Even Queen Victoria did better when she ordered the Marble Arch in London; it is undoubtedly comic, but one grows affectionate towards it. The inhabitants of

179

128 *This 2nd-century mosaic from Tunisia depicts aspects of life on an African estate.*

Timgad did not, I think, give their arch so much as a glance, a year after it was built, but then they were, most of them, Roman legionaries, one of the most extraordinary products of the ancient world.

When Rome began its career of conquest in the time of the Republic, it did so with a citizen army. Its soldiers fought in the summer and returned to their fields or their other occupations in the winter. They lost some of their battles, but won most of them. The price was high: the casualties were very heavy: it was seen that if fighting was to continue (and nobody thought it should stop), then Rome might be depopulated of its active men. By this time, however, Rome had subdued the entire Italian peninsula. The citizen army became a mercenary army, with the actual fighting being done by provincials, in the narrow sense of the word – Italians, that is, but not Romans.

180

When the Empire expanded to truly foreign lands, it found a vast reserve of manpower ready to hand. It was these new, Imperial provincials, who now filled the ranks. They did so, till the end. We have seen how the army made and unmade Emperors. It was these who did it. It was a paradoxical situation. It was as though the old Indian Army of Sikhs and Gurkhas and the rest had elected Edward VII to be King of England on the death of Queen Victoria.

The legionary signed up with the army for twenty years. While he might have to march right across the Empire and even into Italy itself in time of troubles, he usually stayed on the frontiers. This was one of the reasons for his enrolling. At the end of his service, he would be awarded land in the place where he spent most of his life. He would settle down to be a farmer. If his booty had been good, if the donatives had been generous, he could settle down in considerable style. The soldiers in Timgad dreamed of the day when they would have their farms down south from the town. The irrigation works they built can still be seen, strung along the borders of Roman Africa.

Soldiering

But before they could settle down in this happy fashion, they had to do twenty years of soldiering. I use that word because 'fighting' would be wrong. From our schooldays, we have a mental picture of the legions being made up of stern-faced Romans, endlessly marching across excellent roads (which ran quite straight), continuously in combat with ill-organized natives led by men with unpronounceable names, who fought valiantly but ended up by being betrayed. In the early days of the Republic, and even up to the time of Julius Caesar (whose propaganda writings for the home front started the myth), there may have been a little truth in the picture. Romans of Rome were still to be found in the legions, and they were still very mobile. But by the time Timgad came into existence, things were quite different.

In the first place, a legionary stayed for the greater part of his time at home. He would have been recruited from the peasants, the artisans and the unemployed of a frontier district of the Empire; his prime function was to defend this from the barbarians beyond the demarcation line, from whom he would differ very little. When they grew restless he would, indeed, have to march into their territory, but along paths, not roads. He would have to fight a battle or two, but, at least from the time of Trajan onwards, once the battles were won, he would withdraw to his home base.

While on these marches, he would do some 16 miles a day. He would camp during the night. He would have to throw up a perfectly square stockade, inside which, with mathematical precision, the tents were erected. There were two main paths in the camp, crossing at right angles, with other straight paths, also at right angles, leading from it. In fact, camp was a temporary Timgad: Timgad is a permanent camp.

129 *Soldiers blessing the standard, a detail of Trajan's Column in Rome.*

The infantry were the hard core of the army. There was also cavalry, but the horses it rode were too small and light for the cavalry to play much part in the battle tactics. Later in the Empire, when a heavier and more powerful type of horse was bred, the cavalry became more effective. But for most of Roman history the brunt of the fighting fell on the foot-soldier.

It was not until the rise of the motion picture that the legionary was loaded with elaborate armour. The Praetorian Guard sometimes wore ornate breast-plates, but only to look ornamental on parade. The ordinary fighting man sometimes had no other protection than a cuirass of leather. Later, plates of metal were added, both back and front. He wore sandals, not greaves: his shield was a light affair, curved and oblong, consisting of a framework covered with leather, which in turn was covered by a sheet of metal.

His weapons were, in the first stage of an engagement, the *pilum*, a spear with a heavy head which he threw with great force. This done, he retired into a space left in the battle array, and a second line of soldiers came up and threw in their turn. Meantime, the auxiliaries came into play on the wings. There were bands of specialists, such as slingers, or archers. These had been recruited from tribes in the Empire that had developed particular skills on their home soil: the slingers, for instance, came from the Balearics: the archers from the Middle East. They were often allowed to fight in their own native fashion.

The legionaries now joined with the enemy. They used a short, fairly broad sword. This has become almost a symbol of Rome in our minds, but in fact it was invented by the Spanish. The legionaries did not slash about with it when actually locked in combat (though they did against civilians and in massacres). This exposed too much of the body. They thrust with the point. They parried return blows with the shield, their heads being protected by a small iron casque or even just a leather cap.

While the legion could do great damage, it rarely had the overwhelming effect of the Macedonian phalanx, which had sent empires tumbling down before it. The legion won – if it won – because of numbers and persistence. It was generally better disciplined than its opponents, who were fighting for king and country. The legions fought for pay, which was good, and for that farm on the frontier. They fought stubbornly, but sometimes their losses were considerable.

184   130, 131 *Timgad: above, Temple of the Spirit of the Colony;*
below, a street crossing with a view towards the triumphal arch. ⟩

On his expedition to Britain, Septimius Severus lost as many as 50,000 men.

The ones that survived did well. The booty was amassed in a heap and divided according to strict rules of seniority. Prisoners of war had various fates. The old were despatched with the sword, for there were no regulations to protect them. Those of a good physique or with striking looks were enslaved. Their fate was not always dire. A slave who was sent to work in the fields was unlucky: it was a hard life with little prospects. Those who were sent to the towns, especially to Rome, had a good chance of living better than they did in their native forests or villages. From Augustus onwards, the treatment of slaves grew steadily more humane. Brutal punishments were forbidden: we hear of one rich man who seriously injured a slave by striking him over the head with a scabbard. He caused such a scandal that he took the scabbard to a friend and begged his friend to hit him with it.

Slaves in the big cities of the Empire could earn money with which to buy their freedom. Freeing one's slave became what we would call a status symbol. It was so popular a practice that, at one stage, it had to be limited by law. Once a freed man, there was no limit to ambition. Freedmen ran the Imperial palace in Rome, and the Governor's palaces in the provinces. Some grew exceedingly rich.

An arduous part of the legionary's task was laying siege to walled cities. Lines were drawn round the town, out of bow-shot. Siege warfare then began. In Roman hands, it was a steady, plodding business with no heroics. The battlements were kept clear of the enemy by means of siege engines, like the *ballista* which hurled huge rocks, or gigantic bows which fired iron bolts. The walls themselves were attacked by battering rams, worked by men sheltered in large huts covered with clay as a protection against burning arrows, or boiling oil. Other machines drilled holes into the joints of the blocks until they were loosened. If the walls resisted these, tunnels were dug under them. In the siege of Masada, held by the Jews, none of these tactics could be employed, Masada being built on top of a steep hill. The Romans patiently built a ramp of earth 645 feet long and 400 feet high. When it was finished, they charged up it and took the fortress. The remains of this gigantic earthwork can still be seen.

⟨132, 133 *Above, a view of the theatre at Timgad and, below, the triumphal arch as it appeared when one approached the city.*

135, 136 *Bronze statuettes of Roman slaves in pillory.*

When the walls of a city were breached, the city was taken by storm, if, that is, it had not been taken by treachery from within. It was then given over for looting. But if the resistance had been very stubborn, a general massacre would be ordered. The Roman soldiery roamed the streets, cutting down anybody they saw, men, women and children. They broke open houses and slaughtered whole families. They searched out hiding places and cut down their terrified occupants. The killing was quite indiscriminate: the roads were slippery with blood, mutilated corpses lay everywhere. The aim was to create terror, not so much in the captured town, but in neighbouring cities. Should any of them be thinking of defying the Roman army themselves, then this would show them what would happen to them.

The notion that the mass slaughter of unarmed civilians will cause widespread panic is, of course, fundamental to all military thinking even in our own day, when it is practised on a scale impossible in Roman times. The bombing of London, Berlin, Hamburg, and Dresden was firmly believed to be shattering

‹134 *A legionary and a Praetorian; plaster models in the Museo della Civiltà Romana, Rome.*

the morale of the enemy. In no case did it do so. The war was decided only by the defeat of armies in the field. This being so, and widely known, it is curious to observe that military planners still thought the system would work in Indo⁄China, where, again, it did not.

I think, however, that it worked with the Romans. They rarely repeated tactics which had proved unsuccessful. They abandoned the Macedonian phalanx, they refused to be drawn into guerilla warfare, retiring behind walls such as they built in Scotland. They continued, however, to massacre civilians. One reason why it succeeded was that there was no escaping death. There were no shelters which could not be gouged out. There was no escaping into the countryside, for the city was ringed with troops. Soldiers, today, are tried for massacring civilians, unless it be from the air. But for the legionary, systematic butchery was one of the duties for which he was paid, flattered, and rewarded.

This, then, was the fighting life of the men who were sent to live in the disci⁄plined, straight streets of Timgad. It was a purely military existence. Until the time of Septimius Severus, legionaries could not marry. They kept concubines. Their children were brought up outside their camps, and the future of these children was settled from the day of their birth. Rome welcomed the sons of veterans into the ranks of the Army. It therefore follows that the legions must have been multi⁄coloured: but since the Romans had not the slightest trace of colour⁄prejudice, it did not matter in the least, however surprising it may be to us.

The Baths

One of the few human touches in the ruins of Timgad is the profusion of bathing establishments. Thirteen have so far been found. Some of them were merely brothels, no doubt, as they were in Rome and all over its Empire (the Italian word for a house of prostitution was still 'bagno' in our own times), but others had a higher aim. We can best study them by leaving Roman Timgad, going back to Phoenician Leptis Magna, with its freer atmosphere. There we find the majestic ruins of a bathing establishment which was among the biggest in the Roman world.

Entering between massive walls, we look into a perspective of columns and springing arches. Hall after hall opens out as we explore, vault after vault in marvellously fitted stone is above us. Finally, lost, we come out into a square, with sunken pools, and a vast, open space with rounded ends embraced by a graceful colonnade. It is as though we had walked through a royal palace: but it was a palace where every citizen of Leptis was king.

The early Romans, so much admired by the later Romans, did not believe in being overwashed. They took a bath every nine days. As luxury increased, so did the frequency of their ablutions. This was deplored by those who admired the austerity of their forefathers, but what Rome lost in moral strength, it gained in fragrancy. Commodus, the texts record, took eight baths every day, though how he found time between killing all his wild beasts and fighting all his gladiators, it is hard to imagine.

The Romans learned the custom of regular bathing from the Greeks, but in Greece it was a simple affair of sitting in a small tub and having a servant pour

137, 138 *The Hadrianic baths at Leptis Magna. Above, the sunken pool; opposite, a reconstruction of the* frigidarium.

water over you. This was merely to wash off the sweat of the day. The Romans turned the production of perspiration into a way of life. They erected immense marble halls in which to get warm, to get hot, to get boiling hot, then to get freezing cold. The brick cores of two of their establishments, the Baths of Diocletian and those of Caracalla, remain, in ruins, the biggest structures in Rome next to the Colosseum. One of them, in a fragment of its area, nowadays contains a church as big as a cathedral and an enormous museum. The other, in no more than a quarter of its area, contains an open-air opera house seating 20,000 people. The baths at Leptis Magna were built in the time of Hadrian but followed, meticulously, the same design.

The baths were opened at midday. The entrance fee was trivial, and sometimes nothing at all, since some rich man had donated a sum of money to cover the expenses. Every male citizen went, if not every day, then as near to that as he could get. He carried with him a *strigil*, or body-scraper, a little pot of oil, and some towels. Up till the time of Septimius Severus, he had to buy the oil. Severus ordered that it should be free, at the expense of the state.

192

139–141 *Left, mosaic at the entrance to the baths in Timgad; left below, a mosaic sign from the women's baths; opposite, the* tepidarium.

142 *Air view of the Baths of Caracalla in Rome.*

194

This entry into the baths grew into an exercise in snobbery. It was 'not done' for the upper classes to carry their own *strigil*. A string of slaves was required, the more the better. Some men in the peak of fashion had the slaves carry them into the baths, for it was *chic*, during the height of the Empire, to be thought incapable of doing anything oneself, except to have sex and eat. One man is recorded as being in his carrying chair, and anxiously inquiring of his body-servant, 'Am I sitting up?'

This is an extreme. The normal thing was to take some exercise, after which the body was rubbed with oil, which had to be scraped off. The bather now went into an ornate chamber which was cunningly heated by hot air flowing under the floor and inside the walls. Here he sat, conversing with his friends until he was well warmed up. He passed under the arches we have seen to a second hall. In the centre of this was a basin bubbling with steaming water. Here he got hotter than ever. If he chose, he could go on still further to a room in which the atmosphere resembled that of the hottest room in our own Turkish baths. From either of these two last rooms, he went straight to an open-air swimming pool and plunged into cold water.

After that, he strolled about, or sat in alcoves, talking to his friends. The baths were surrounded by shops which sold wine, sweetmeats and snacks. He could, if he liked, get drunk, though it was not considered very elegant. At about half-past two, he went home to dinner.

It was largely a male institution. The men went naked: as for the women, they either had separate hours in which to bathe, or had establishments of their own, sharing the furnaces of the men's department, but cut off from it. But for a woman to go to the baths at all was considered rather middle-class. The aristocratic woman stayed at home, where she had luxurious steam baths of her own and an army of slaves to attend her.

When Rome was at the height of its power, its subjects scrambled to copy Roman ways. Baths arose everywhere; and were used in the Roman fashion. But when the baths at Leptis Magna were excavated, a curious statue was discovered. I find it fascinating, because it is evidence of what the Phoenicians really thought of the Romans, deep in their traders' hearts.

<143 *The Baths of Caracalla : floor mosaics representing athletes and their trainer.*

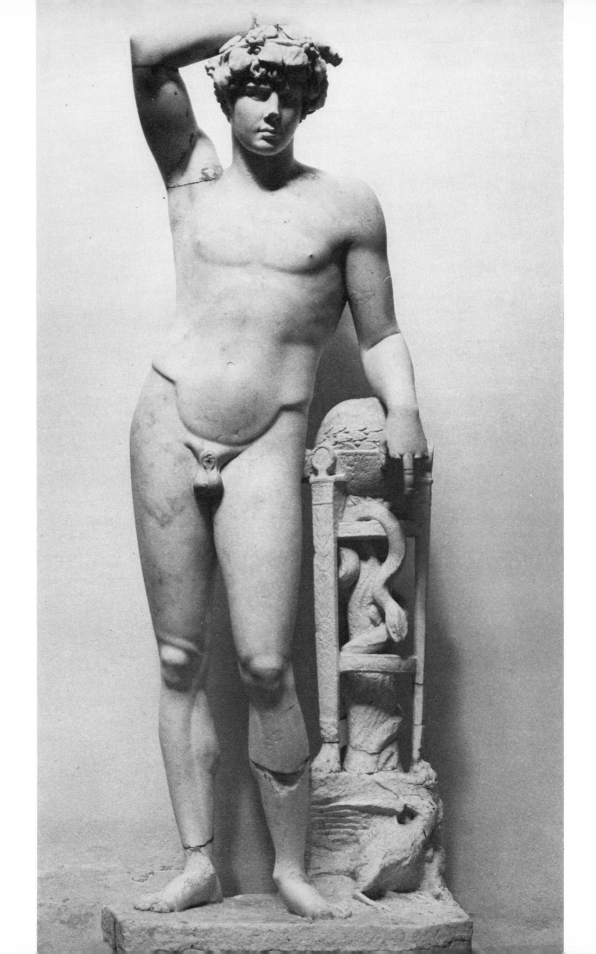

The Triumph of the East

All public baths in the Roman Empire were decorated with statues. These statues were either made by Greeks, or were copies of Greek statues. The Romans had little creative ability in the plastic arts, but they had early on decided that they did not need any; the Greeks had said the final word in the matter. They also lacked the gift of creating religious myths: the early religion of the Romans was an abstract and superstitious affair, suited for peasants. The Romans once again turned to the Greeks, and took over Olympus, changing some names, but not the stories. The only myth they invented was that dead Emperors, and even their wives, could become gods and goddesses when they died.

The statue found in the baths at Leptis Magna was of the god Apollo, mediocre in workmanship and a commonplace specimen of official art, except for one thing. Its face had been cut away and the features of a boy put in its place. The boy was a portrait of Antinous, the young Bithynian slave with whom the Emperor had fallen desperately in love. While there was some criticism in Rome, on the whole Hadrian's passion was accepted. Pederasty, like good sculpture, was after all Greek, and thus cultured. In the Mediterranean world outside Rome, the love affair was more sympathetically received. Antinous became famous.

He died in a boating accident on the Nile. Whether he was drowned by jealous courtiers, whether he committed suicide to protect Hadrian from some prophecy, or whether his death was a banal accident, we cannot say: all three explanations hold the field. Whatever the cause, Hadrian's grief was spectacular. He arranged for the boy to be declared a god and caused statues to be raised to him throughout the Empire. He even founded a town in Egypt called Antinoöpolis. Cults arose around the boy's memory.

‹144 *The statue of Antinous.*

It is clear that the good merchants of Leptis Magna did not throw themselves into this furor with unmeasured enthusiasm. If the Emperor really wanted a statue of his favourite boy, he should have one, of course, but partly second-hand. I find it a thought-provoking relic.

What was it like for these seafaring men, bold enough to sail round Africa, to have the statue of an Emperor's lover looking down at them each day when they went to the baths? Perhaps the question rises in my mind because of my boyhood days in India. Then, too, the country was dotted with statues of emperors and empresses, often paid for by rich merchants. There was one of Edward VII; none, as I remember, of his mistress, Lily Langtry; but such was the profound indifference of everybody to these effigies, that had there been, nobody would have cared.

I think it was there that I learned how lightly men hold liberty. The man who has nothing to say is not greatly concerned with freedom of speech. The man who can barely govern his wife has no burning desire to sit in the councils of the nation. The man who knows no history is content to let other people make it. A man prefers to be ruled by one of his own kind, but if things become intolerable, he will willingly swap a fool for a foreigner.

Thus it was in India. After centuries of mismanagement, of petty wars, of gigantic corruption, there was order in the land. The country ran. It ran until its foreign masters exhausted themselves in the First World War, and nearly destroyed themselves in the Second. When that happens, when the foreigner is too tired or too confused to rule, then is the time for the birth of such noble ideals as freedom, independence and liberty. They are, after all, inescapable.

From the point of view of Leptis Magna, the Empire meant that business prospered. Taxes had to be paid, but with the trade routes open and kept open by the soldiers, money could be made to pay them. Emperors came and went, some good, some bad, some preposterous. But there was a permanent civil service. It was corrupt, but that only worried the man who had not enough money for bribery. For a businessman, communications are vital. Under the Empire, they were excellent. The Imperial post not only carried sentences of death, it carried letters. Septimius Severus, well aware of the importance of this service, made it free, something we are far from achieving in our own times.

There was one other thing – and here my Indian analogy breaks down and must be discarded. In the early days of the Empire, its rulers, nominal (like the Senate), or real (like the Emperors), were Roman, of Roman stock. But Trajan and Hadrian had come from Spain. As the Roman world widened, so did its mind. The Romans possessed a gift denied to the other builders of empires – the British, the Spaniards, the Portuguese. They had no racial prejudice. When Caracalla extended Roman citizenship to all free men in the Empire, he was only completing a process which had been going on for nearly two centuries.

Leptis, then, continued to trade and make money in the Pax Romana, and if the soldiery occasionally made a desert to keep that peace, it did not happen in Leptis or hundreds of other towns around the Mediterranean. The Phoenicians, after the disaster of Carthage, once more quietly survived.

More than survived, because they witnessed their triumph. Leptis gave Rome an Emperor. The Phoenicians had come from the eastern Mediterranean. Severus took to himself a Syrian wife. Eastern ways, eastern philosophies took hold of Rome, until, for better or worse, the Semites saw Elagabalus install a Semitic Baal in the heart of Rome.

I must now turn to a Syrian city for the rest of the story.

Palmyra

About the time when the Phoenicians were building their cities along the eastern coast of the Mediterranean, another tribe of Semites had settled far inland in what is now called Syria. They were the Arameans. They had no special gifts, like that of the Phoenicians for sailing boats, except that they had a singularly good eye for siting a town. They found an oasis on the edge of the desert and here they built Tadmor, a city that was to become a legend.

Tadmor was on the great caravan routes. There was the road that led from far India and China, through Persia. There was the other route that came up the Red Sea and crossed Syria. There was the route to the shores of the Mediterranean. The caravans came from all these directions and rested at the oasis. Here, conveniently, came the buyers from the West, or the carriers, like the Phoenicians. Here, the gold, the jewels, the silks and the spices were sold and bought; Tadmor saved both Eastern and Western merchants long and fatiguing journeys. It also made its founders rich.

The Arameans put a tax on all the goods that exchanged hands. It was not a mere piratical imposition. The Arameans supplied water from their springs, some of it with medicinal qualities. They organized and disciplined the constant comings and goings of the caravans. They housed their beasts and masters. They provided the market place. The Chief of the Caravans and the Chief of the Market were among their most prominent citizens.

As was proper for men who dealt with all the world, the language they spoke was clear and easy to understand. It slowly spread over all Syria and the Jewish kingdoms which bordered on Syria. It was spoken in Jerusalem, by one man in particular who has made sure that their tongue has survived to this day.

145 Palmyra: a portico over the road through which wild beasts were driven into the theatre. ⟩

148 *A colonnaded street in Palmyra.*
⟨146, 147 *Above, the Temple of Bel at Palmyra;*
below, the remaining pillars of the colonnade of the Forum.

When scholars search for the meaning behind the words of Jesus of Nazareth, they must study Aramaic.

Tadmor grew more and more splendid till the legend arose that it had been built by King Solomon, for it seemed impossible that it could have been built by merchants.

The Roman Empire arose. The Romans cast covetous eyes on the wealth of Tadmor (particularly Mark Antony), but they left it in peace. The Arameans had become middlemen in another sense. They now stood between two rival empires, that of the Persians and that of the Romans. Both were bitter enemies and often at war. Tadmor once again made money out of it. She had treaties with the Romans that made her part of the Empire, but she was so important that she did not lose her independence. She maintained it by her peaceful ways. She lost it in the end because ambition drove her inhabitants out of the paths of peace to that of a disastrous war.

Meantime, her name had changed. The Romans, mistaking one Semitic word for another, thought 'Tadmor' meant palm trees. Since the oasis was thick with them, it seemed probable. They called Tadmor 'Palmyra', a name which has gathered no less romance around it than the first one.

During all this time, the Palmyrenes maintained the friendliest of relations with the Romans. Hadrian visited it in AD 130, and honoured it by giving the city his own name. It now became Hadriana Palmyra. Septimius Severus made it a provincial city of the Empire with all the privileges this entailed.

Then came Caracalla and Elagabalus and Alexander Severus. The soldiers ruled the Empire and, as we have seen, disorder began to spread. After Alexander Severus, the descent became faster, until at last, complete anarchy reigned. The Palmyrenes rebelled, lost, and their city was laid waste. It was rebuilt, but fortune had deserted it. Its trade declined, its inhabitants left. The followers of Mohammed took the town without a blow. They used its great monuments as building stone. The chief temple became a fortress and a mosque. Palmyra was forgotten by the world. The sand from the desert drifted in, the palm trees withered. In the end, the only inhabitants of Palmyra were a handful of Arabs who had built hovels among the ruins.

149 *Tower tombs on the outskirts of Palmyra.*

Here they were seen by the European travellers that passed by. Such travellers were very rare: by now the trade routes had changed. An Italian, Pietro della Valle, saw it in the seventeenth century. In 1630 the great traveller, Tavernier, came across it, and then some English merchants. The squalid Bedouin locked them up, demanding ransom.

Then in the eighteenth century, a great curiosity about the past grew up in the European mind. Archaeology began, tentatively, and tales spread of this ruined and remote city sinking in the sand. Expeditions were sent out. Digging began: the mosque was pulled down: inscriptions were deciphered. But down to today, Palmyra is still largely unexplored. An air of mystery hangs over its ruins. They do not seem to be real, like the ruins of Leptis or Timgad. They emerge from the desert like some abandoned film-set. Perhaps the Arabs have the just phrase to describe it. It was not built by men, they say, but by some djinn.

The visitor approaches Palmyra through a shallow valley. It is lined with tombs that, at the very beginning, bring that air of strangeness that never leaves

150 *Palmyrene soldiers, fragment
of a 2nd-century relief.*

one. Not that there is anything bizarre in Palmyra: its ruins are not incomprehensible, like those of Mexico. Instead, there is an air of everything being a little different. However many ruins one has visited, there is none quite like this.

The tombs, for instance. They are stone towers, some low, some high and massive. They have small windows like those in the medieval fortresses in Italy; yet the towers are grimmer and more forbidding than the Italian towers; and that is not to be wondered at, for they are fortresses of the dead.

It seems that the Palmyrenes buried their dead, in the ground. Each family that could afford it carved out a catacomb, with niches and shelves on which the bodies were put. When Christian catacombs became full, tunnels and galleries were dug out to increase their size. The Palmyrenes, however, wanted something grander than rabbit-runs. They built towers over the catacombs, decorating them with paintings and carvings. Here again, there were shelves and niches,

151, 152 *Funerary relief of a married couple in Palmyra, and the funerary bust of a woman (right).*

153 *The elaborate Tomb of the Three Brothers, Palmyra.*

so that the tower became a sort of apartment house for the departed. Like all apartment houses, they were useful to own in times of trouble. In one of these towers an inscription has been found which says that the original owners, a family, sold the upper storeys to someone else – at a time which, as we know from other indications, was one of financial recession in Palmyra.

It was plainly the ambition of all Palmyrenes with the money to have a tower, the size of it marking one's social status. One of the tombs had places for four hundred bodies: others were planned on a similar scale, but never finished, the owners having run out of funds. Others lavished money on carved friezes and paintings. One, the Tomb of the Three Brothers, is particularly rich in decoration. The style is haunting, like all Palmyrene art.

A brief climb up the side of the valley, and all Palmyra lies before you. It looks like the skeleton of some unimaginably vast monster, its bones sticking up through the sand. There is the long, curving spine, a suggestion of broken limbs, and far away is the skeleton of the head. The bones are columns, hundreds of them, some lying on the ground, others standing in serried lines. A closer,

154, 155 *Above, an air view of the ruins of Palmyra, and, below, a plan showing the extent of the city.*

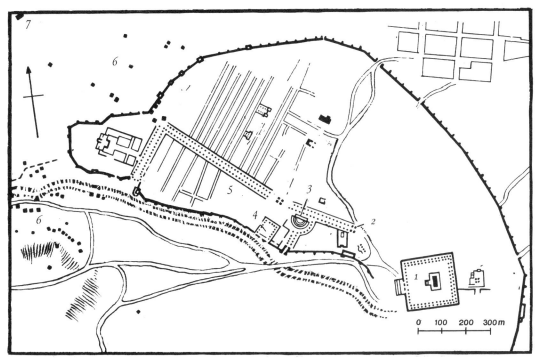

1 The Temple of Bel
2 Triumphal Arch
3 Theatre
4 Agora
5 Colonnade
6 Tower Tombs
7 Ottoman Castle

156–158 *The triumphal arch at Palmyra and details of Palmyrene pillars and capitals.*

longer look, and the image of the monster fades. You distinguish streets and squares, but with the stones wildly tumbled about. The Arabs said a djinn had built it, and just so it seems: a wilful djinn, who, when his work of sticking these columns in the sand was done, lost his temper with his master. He kicked and trampled about, destroying most of his work, grew tired and went back to his bottle or his lamp. Then the sand of the desert blew for centuries, covering some of the havoc, but leaving enough – just enough– to show that the djinn had built a splendid, shining city.

The ruins of Palmyra are sparse: but that is what gives them a beauty unique in the world. Elsewhere, archaeologists have dug about, as is their duty, uncovering, for the most part, only the empty shells of shops and houses. The great monuments that have been visible through the ages soon become surrounded by a warren of topless boxes from which everything of interest has been removed and taken to museums. With that, something of the grandeur of the ruins inevitably disappears.

That has not happened to Palmyra. It has been little studied and explored. Apart from the huts of the Bedouin, it looks very much the same as it did when those Europeans I have named first came across it. It is possible to imagine for a while that one has discovered it oneself.

Stretching right across the city – the spine of the skeleton of the monster – is Palmyra's most famous monument, the Great Colonnade. It is over a kilometre in length and a large number of the columns are still standing. They are huge affairs, over nine metres high and nearly a metre thick. They are set close together, like Bernini's colonnade in front of St Peter's. Their capitals are richly carved in the Corinthian style, much worn by sandstorms. The driving sand has also worn some of their bases, eating them away, giving them a fragile look as though a high wind could snap them. About half-way up on each is a small ledge. On these once stood statues of the town's most famous citizens. All have gone, but this immense corridor of columns is a lasting monument to how rich they were.

It is a living street. It has not been drawn with a ruler like the streets of Timgad. The long line is broken to make a refreshing angle. Two archways relieved the eye: one, with four entrances, has disappeared except for its foundations. The other is still there, a graceful affair with one central arch, and

159 *Overleaf, a view of the Great Colonnade leading towards the triumphal arch.*

160 *The Temple of Bel.*

two side arches. On both sides of this colonnade street were once shops and trading offices. It is easy to fill it in one's imagination with all the bustle, the noise, the laughter and the quarrels, such as one hears in the Street called Straight in nearby Damascus. But this, with its columns, its statues, its carved capitals, must have been much more noble.

At the end of the colonnade – not *precisely* at the end, as it would be in a Roman town, but off-angled – there is the great Temple of Bel. From a distance, the ruin seems familiar enough, at least for anyone who has seen the temples of Rome, of Sicily and Greece. There are the usual rows of columns of the peristyle, or outer surround of the shrine, high up on a platform. There seem to be rather a large number of them.

It is only when the visitor has mounted the front steps and wandered among the ruins that a sense of strangeness sets in, a disorientation. Here are the familiar columns with their capitals, but arranged in what bears down upon one in a *foreign* manner.

The temples of the Greeks and Romans have a frank air. They are open. A free wind blows through their columns. They invite the worshipper to enter, after he has watched his sacrifice being made on the altar outside. A temple is the house of the god, but an open house. Here, in the temple of a Semitic god, we are in a different world. Pacing the ruins, studying the plan, the visitor begins to understand that this temple was a hidden place. It was surrounded by a high wall, decorated with pilasters, and pierced by three gates. Much of that barrier was torn down by the Arab conquerors, to turn the temple into a fort. A bastion built of the remains is still to be seen. But, when it was complete, the temple must have already had the look of a fortress. We are a long way from the Parthenon and near to the closed courtyards of Solomon's Temple. The gods that dwelt in these Eastern shrines were held in greater awe than ever the Greeks and the Romans bestowed on their deities. As, slowly, the shape of this temple pieces itself together in one's mind, it becomes easier to see why the Syrian Elagabalus walked backwards before his conical stone when he brought it to Rome.

Inside these walls, on all four sides, was a portico. On three sides the columns stood in double rows, giving a spacious walk: on the side of the entrance, they

were in single file. Many of them are standing and it is these that give the impression at first blush of being the temple. Their capitals are rough, as though something had happened to prevent their being carved with the acanthus leaves that one expects. In fact, the leaves were there: but the Palmyrenes were so rich that they could afford to have them made of bronze. They made a fine booty for the invaders.

Inside all this splendour stood the *cella*, or shrine proper of the god. The front was decorated with reliefs, finely carved. One of these must have taken the fancy of the Moslem conquerors: it shows women wearing veils. They are portrayed by means of strong, swirling lines ending in spirals. They, too, add to the

161, 162 *Above, the interior of the Temple of Bel, and (right) a detail of the outer walls.*

163 *This detail of a relief from the Temple of Bel shows veiled women at the right,* c. *AD 32.*

strangeness. No Greek or Roman sculptor could have conceived these almost abstract figures. Arp and Brancusi come to mind irresistibly.

Inside, there is the niche which held the statue of Bel, and there are two niches for his companions – Jarhibol, the sun-god, and Agli-bol, the god of the moon. In one of the niches is a stone ceiling carved with a circular band of figures, all very bold. They are the familiar signs of the zodiac. What part astrology played in Palmyra's religion, we cannot be sure. We do know, however, that eating had its place.

From time to time, the priests of Bel would arrange banquets in honour of the god. The Palmyrenes would provide the food in the shape of sacrificial animals. The steps up which they were led can still be seen. Tickets were issued to the more distinguished citizens, and they were much sought after. When all the privileged were assembled, the statue of the god was carried round the porticoes in a grand procession, and then the banquet began. Standing in this secret and solemn place, it is impossible to think that the feast was a very jolly affair. Bel, like Tanit in Carthage, must have been a deity to fear.

We return down the Great Colonnade, which, after the time spent in the massive ruins of the Temple of Bel, seems to fill out and become less skeletal. We find a theatre: it is much the same as that of Leptis, but more ruined. The sand has done its damage and the outlines of its several parts are softened. Boldness and grandeur come back with the ruin next door.

220

It is the Agora, or market place. It is enclosed by enormous walls, which in turn are surrounded by a portico. Many of the columns are standing. Here, too, each had its console on which stood a statue of a celebrity. The statues are gone, but the inscriptions have remained. It was a grand parade of two hundred famous men. On the north side were ranged the statues of the high officials. On the east side, facing the Senate House, were famous Senators. On the west were military commanders. All this might be Rome: but it is the south side that tells us we are in another world. Here were the statues of leaders *of caravans*.

That would have been unthinkable in Rome. The city would have died without its merchants, and, indeed, when they stopped coming and tied their

164 *Relief from the court of the Temple of Bel which represents Bel in the centre, and the lesser gods Jarhibol and Agli-bol on each side of him.*

ships up in Byzantium instead of Ostia, Rome withered away. But never, in all its history, did Rome rank a merchant with Senators and soldiers. It was – and is – a long-lasting prejudice. Westminster Abbey is cluttered with statues of the great, or their tombstones. Kings, politicians, and commanders are there: even poets have their corner. But there are no merchant adventurers. America's greatness was built on business, yet there are no statues of businessmen on the green lawns of Washington, D.C. Here, in Palmyra, such men were honoured, with great common sense. It is as though, between the memorials of Lincoln and Jefferson, another classic temple had been built to honour the father of the greatest caravan of all time, Henry Ford.

It is a pity that the Palmyrenes did not stick to their common sense. The Agora is in ruins, but they were not made by an enemy. Seized with a desire to be heroes, the Palmyrenes rose in revolt. The stones of the Agora were torn down by the Palmyrenes themselves, in a last desperate attempt to defend the city. Of that revolt, and the woman who led it, I shall tell in its place.

165 *Funerary bust of a camel driver from Palmyra,* c. *AD 140–60.*

166 *A view of the Ottoman castle on its hill above Palmyra.*

At the far end of the Great Colonnade, on the confines of the city, rises the most telling monument in Palmyra, not for its size, but the drama of its setting. The façade of a temple with a broken pediment rises from a jumble of fallen blocks. There is nothing left behind the façade: one looks straight through at a great rocky hill that towers above it, dwarfing it. The hill is crowned with a lowering Ottoman castle, built by Palmyra's Moslem conquerors. It sits up there, in the sunlight, like a beast crouched over the bones of its prey.

The columns are those of a funerary temple, a place, that is, where banquets were held in memory of the dead, who may have been buried within its precincts. It is gaunt enough now, until one looks among the fallen stones, or at the one carved column that remains upright. Then one sees the richness of its adornment. Spirals of plants are carved in a sort of ordered tropical jungle. The Romans and the Greeks were masters at carving such reliefs. In their hands, they were chaste. Here they are lush. There is, it seems, a desire not only to make something beautiful to take the spectator's eye: there is a desire to knock it out. It is a show-off: looking at it, one can think of nothing but the sheer time and expense that were spent on it. It is possible that if we could see classical temples as they were, with their painted statues, golden tiles and decorations of heavy bronze, we would get the same feeling. Here, we do not have to use our historical imaginations. We can run our fingers over and under and in and out of all the luxury.

223

I have spoken briefly of the remarkable sculpture of the Palmyrenes. The rich decoration of the funerary temple is a good introduction to its qualities. They are virtues which can, at first, repel. On close study – and remembering the honours done to caravan masters – they have an attraction which cannot be found elsewhere.

A great number of portrait statues have been unearthed. The best must nowadays be searched out in the museums in Palmyra or Damascus, but some are still on the site. Almost all of them have one thing in common, and that is their boldness. The strokes of the chisel are deep. The shapes are rounded, almost to fatness. The eyes, carved to a formula, stare out brazenly. The port of the head is never modest; in statues of women, it tends to arrogance. Most of the women display heavy jewels, all faithfully copied by the sculptor. Looking at them, I am reminded of the women who bulge and glitter at the opening night of La Scala in Milan. They, too, have money, and do not mind if you know it.

Yet there is something beyond mere ostentation. The fixed stare is hypnotic. The eyes are looking at you, very directly at you. But there is a hieratic indifference to you. At first, you are inclined to dismiss it as a provincial woodenness on the part of the artist. He had been taught to do it that way, the only way he knew.

Then echoes begin to stir in the mind. You have seen that stare before, that hieratic look, that distancing of the gaze. Soon, other images begin to float between you and the statue: the great Byzantine mosaics in Ravenna, in Monreale, in Rome. There, this style has been brought to an awesome perfection. There is no other way to portray Christ Pantocrator, or the Emperor and Empress of Byzantium.

It was this Syrian art which gave rise to that of Constantinople: for that metropolis was flooded with Syrians. The art was, of course, enormously developed, but its roots lie here. They are roots which gave rise to a marvellous tree. Classical art, the art of Greece and Rome, died with the Dark Ages, and was forgotten. When the light of culture began to glimmer again, it was to the Byzantines that the artists turned. From their stiff copies of the Byzantine style – or attempts at copies – came the flowering of the Middle Ages, and not till the early years of the Renaissance did classical art return. During that long interval, with all its glories, the sculptors of Europe, all unknowingly, had their roots here, in Palmyra.

⟨167 *Bust of a woman from Palmyra, early 3rd century AD.*

A View from Palmyra

Let us study what these comfortable, rich people saw when they looked at the world around them in the year AD 236. They were part of the Roman Empire, but it was a greatly changed Empire from the times when Hadrian had given Palmyra his name. It was now ruled by Maximinus, the physical giant who had taken the fancy of Septimius Severus: or, to be nearer the truth, it was ruled by the soldiers. Buying the throne by bribing the legions had now become an established practice. As a result, for the first time in history, the Empire was being run by a barbarian.

Maximinus was uncouth; it might be imagined that, once in his great office, he would have made an attempt to change his ways. He did not. Instead, like a true peasant, he nursed a bitter hatred of the polished townee. While a peasant must content himself with being surly to his betters, an Emperor could kill. This Maximinus did. On the barest of excuses, or with none at all, he slaughtered Senators and men whose education was better than his. He was an unmitigated tyrant who acted from naked envy. He was so strong that he could break a horse's leg with a blow of his fist: and that was the only sort of virtue that he aimed to be praised for. He needed money and more money to keep the soldiers happy, as did all the Emperors after Septimius had set the pace. But he exacted it from the provinces with such brutality that one, Africa, could bear it no longer, and broke into open revolt.

Looking across the bounds of one Empire, the Palmyrenes could see another. A new and vigorous dynasty, the Sassanids, had seized the vast territories of the Persian Empire. They boded no good for Palmyra. They swore to drive the Romans out of Syria into the Mediterranean; with a huge army at their disposal, it did not seem impossible that they could do it. As good traders, the Palmyrenes kept on good terms with them, but watchfully. They had their trade routes to protect, and it seemed that the Sassanids would cut them. They were developing routes of their own to deflect the wealth of the Palmyrenes into their own purses. To turn back this menace, the Palmyrenes needed the support of an army equally as big as that of the Persians. This could come only from Rome. Meantime, the caravans came and went: the Palmyrenes paid their taxes to the barbarian Emperor; unlike the Africans, they lay low.

The rebellious Africans had chosen an old, honest man to be the Emperor. He begged to be spared the dangerous honour, but, threatened by the rebels, he accepted. The Senate in Rome, for once, acted with decision. They had little alternative, for it was clear that the savage the soldiers had put upon the throne would destroy them. They acclaimed the old man and his son the rightful Emperor of Rome. Thus, Gordian I and Gordian II entered the list of the rulers of the Empire. Their reign was to last twenty-two days. Gordian I attempted to remove a corrupt Governor of Numidia. When he rose in revolt, Gordian and his son went out to war. Gordian II was killed in battle, and his father, in grief, committed suicide.

What happened next is so vertiginous I shall inevitably make the reader's head spin: but the story must be told: it perfectly illustrates the state of the Empire.

When Maximinus heard of the choice of the Gordians, he flew into ungovernable rage and set out with his army for Italy and Rome, places which, till now, he had not deigned to visit. The Senate hastily chose *two* other Emperors from among themselves, Maximus and Balbinus, at which the people of Rome also flew into an ungovernable rage. They rioted. The soldiers joined them. When the two brand-new Emperors went up to the Temple of Jupiter on the Capitol to make the ritual sacrifices, the mob invaded the hill, demanding another Gordian. There was one available, the grandson of the old man. The Senate, terrified, produced him and he was named Caesar, a subsidiary title to that of Emperor, but one which assured him of the succession, if anything could be assured in that tumultuous time.

Meantime, the enraged Maximinus and his army had entered Italy. They laid siege to the town of Aquilae, because the inhabitants remained loyal. Loyal to what, it is difficult to say, but perhaps it was to the memory of the now vanished grandeur of Rome. Their resistance was stubborn. Maximinus' soldiers began to starve. Then came an added disaster. Plague broke out among the troops, a disease which, in the coming years, was to prove a worse scourge even than the Praetorians and Emperors. Exasperated, the soldiers took that sort of political action to which they were accustomed – they killed Maximinus.

For once it seemed that the assassination was a good thing. The Empire was now ruled by two civilized men (Balbinus was even a poet), who had been legally chosen by the Senate. They had chosen *two* Emperors in the hope that each man would keep the other in check, thus avoiding one Emperor becoming yet another tyrant. It had the makings of a sensible arrangement. At last, it seemed, some sanity was coming back to Rome.

But a sensible arrangement was the last thing that the soldiers wanted. They had tasted power, to say nothing of money, and they had no intention of losing either. *They* made Emperors, not the Senate. The two Emperors duly quarrelled, as was expected. The soldiers bided their time. One day, when all Rome was at one of its favourite amusements, they invaded the palace. The Emperors, hearing the noise, came from their respective apartments, met, and discussed what to do. Naturally, they disagreed, but not for long. The soldiers seized them, stripped them, and drove them with blows and insults through the streets of Rome. They killed them, leaving their bleeding, naked bodies by the roadside.

Things were back to normal. The soldiers were once more in control. They proceeded to choose another master of the Empire, selecting, after much debate, Gordian. At the time of his elevation to the purple, Gordian was thirteen years old. It may seem strange that the soldiers should choose a child but the Gordians, it should be noted, were very rich.

Clearly, a schoolboy could not govern an Empire. A heterogeneous group ran the world – relatives, freedmen, and particularly eunuchs. Soon one man emerged, Timesitheus. He was probably honest and efficient. If he was, his reward is that we know nothing about him.

But now attention was turned away from Rome, to Syria and the East. The Persians were actively following out their plan of throwing the Romans into the sea. They threatened the key city of Antioch: something had to be done. The boy-emperor solemnly declared war by opening the gates of the Temple of Janus, a ceremony which for centuries marked the fact that the might of Rome was about to be deployed. The legions, with young Gordian at their head, marched to Syria.

Timesitheus died, from that rare cause of mortality among men in power near the Emperor – an illness. Now something happened that would have set tongues wagging in Palmyra. The Emperor appointed Julius Verus Philippus to the vacant post, that of the all-powerful Praetorian Prefect. The Latinized name conceals the surprise of the appointment. Philip was an Arab. The historian Edward Gibbon remarks, with distaste, that this meant that Philip was, by race and nurture, a robber. The Arabs did, in fact, rob the caravans, if they were not paid for protection. But they also led them. The worthies who were honoured on the brackets in the market place of Palmyra now had a son who ran the world beside the Emperor.

Beside, that is, a mere boy, and in the middle of a powerful army. When some foodships did not arrive, Philip saw his chance. He told the troops that the scarcity of provisions was due to Gordian's incompetence, though Philip may have contrived the shortage himself. The soldiers, as ever, took the matter into their own hands. That left little doubt in the boy's mind as to what was in store for him. He begged the soldiers to spare him. He offered to step down in rank, to become a Caesar or even a Prefect. These arrangements being too complicated for the soldierly mind, the troops murdered him. Philip the Arabian was declared Emperor. Philip had done his best: he had asked the troops to spare the boy. But they, having elected a stripling to the throne, now declared that he was too young for so great a post, especially, no doubt, since they believed he had neglected to keep their bellies filled. Philip gave the order to have the boy killed, writing to the Senate that he had died from natural causes. The Senate confirmed the Arabian in his emperorship. They could, after all, do little else.

Philip the Arabian turned out to be, at least on the face of things, more Roman than the Romans themselves. He treated the impotent Senate with the respect due to its long history. Instead of cutting off Senators' heads, a thing to which, as we have seen, they had grown accustomed, he sought their friendship, and

168–170 Three coins of Philip the Arabian, commemorating the secular games.

171 Philip the Arabian (AD 244–49), a contemporary portrait bust.

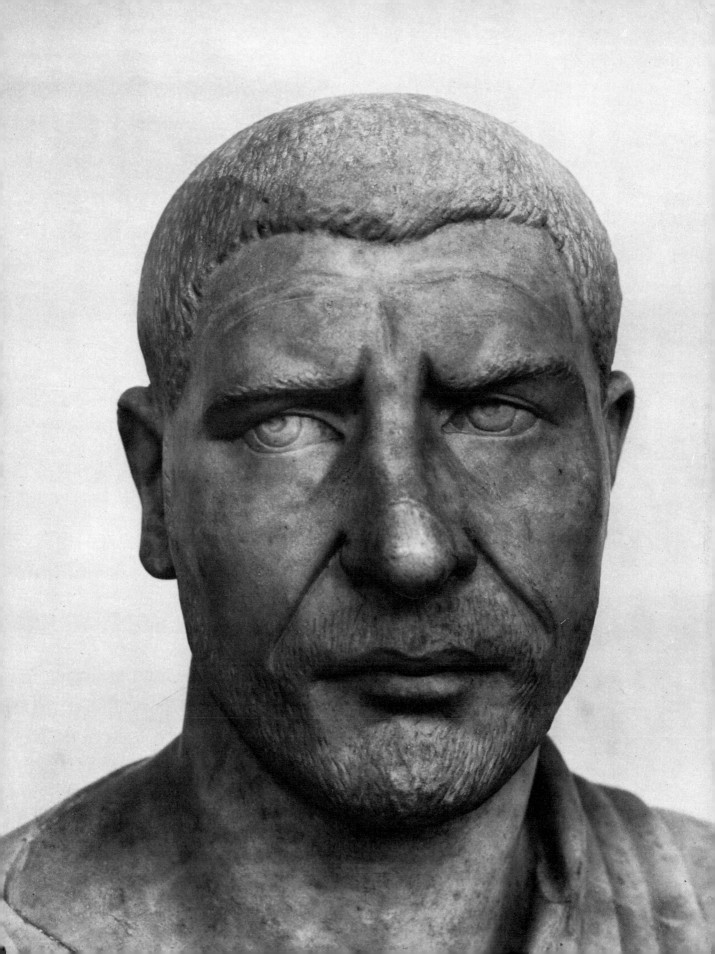

obtained it. He made a favourable peace with the Persians: he celebrated the secular games, not only with magnificence, but with a faithful following of the ancient customs.

The secular games had their origin in the Romans' reverence for their own history. They were held only once in every hundred (or one hundred and ten) years, as the Sybilline books of prophecy commanded. They had a peculiar solemnity, because nobody (or very few) would claim to have seen them before. Rome was now a thousand years old, so Philip's celebration had a particular importance.

All Rome gathered round the traditional field in the Campus Martius, down by the Tiber. The ceremonies were held at night-time, amidst a blaze of torches. Sacrifices were made. A chorus of twenty-seven noble youths and twenty-seven virgins sang hymns invoking the gods to maintain Rome's glory and to aid her citizens to remain true to the virtues of their forefathers. After three days, rejoicing began. For a week, there were spectacles in the amphitheatre, on which Philip lavished money.

It was all quintessentially Roman. Strangers were excluded, lest they spoil things by their presence. Rome, it seemed, had returned to her noble self.

But strangers were pressing on all the frontiers, soon to burst across them: and a stranger sat on the throne of the Caesars. In Palmyra, none of these things went unobserved.

The Empire Collapses

As Septimius Severus had advised, the Emperors who followed him had one thought in mind – to bribe the soldiery. It was a system which enfeebled the army and ruined the citizens. Soldiers who bathed in a shower of gold at every stroke of the assassin's sword were not likely to be hardy fighting men. Pampered by Emperors in fear of their lives, they could not be disciplined. Who was there to do it? Certainly not their generals. These aimed at popularity like any demo-cratic politician of our own times. It was the one road that led to power. Inevitably, the soldiers grew lax. The frontiers were no longer guarded by hard-bitten fighters, proud of a thousand-year-old tradition of invincibility. They were guarded by men absorbed solely in their own personal interests. That is, the frontiers were guarded poorly indeed. Behind them lay all the spoils of Empire: in front of them hoards of hungry barbarians, with nothing but a demoralized army to stop them crossing and taking their fill.

To the barbarian the Empire was a tempting prize: but in fact it was already bankrupt. The insensately huge donations handed out to the soldiers by each temporary Emperor had emptied the treasury. Merciless exactions had by now ruined the taxpayer, who not only had to maintain the irresponsible extra-vagance of the Emperors, but, each time the barbarians probed, had also to take on the additional burden of financing defensive wars.

Into this black picture swept a new and unforeseen disaster – the plague. In the year AD 250 the disease broke out in Egypt. It swept rapidly across the Mediterranean and up the Italian peninsula. There was no remedy for it. It raged for fifteen years. At one time, in Rome itself, it was carrying off five thousand people a day.

Philip had died in battle. Beside the fate of other Emperors, it seemed almost a death by natural causes. He was not fighting the barbarians, but a usurper, elected as usual by his troops. His name was Decius: for a fleeting two years Rome was ruled by a sensible man. He made some statesmanlike reforms: he attempted to restore respect for the traditions of Rome. Unfortunately for his renown in history, one of the measures he took was to insist that the growing sect of Christians should make sacrifice to the gods. When they refused to do this, he persecuted them. Under cruel, but customary tortures, many Christians stood firm: many, on the other hand, did not. The Church is founded on the blood of martyrs, and the Decian persecution figures largely in its history. But Decius was not attacking their faith. To him, they were no more than yet another of the Eastern sects which had fascinated the Romans. He was merely attempting to keep the disintegrating state in some semblance of order.

Then the Goths moved across the Danube. Decius went to meet them. A battle was fought at Aprittus, in the Balkans. Decius lost his life in a bog. He was led into the bog by the treachery of Gallus, who, for his cleverness, was proclaimed Emperor by the troops.

Neither Gallus nor his successor, Aemilianus, need detain us; Gallus reigned two years: his usurper, three months. Both were elected by the troops, both were slain by them. We must pause, however, over their successor, Valerian. It has been his sad fate to become the grotesque symbol of the nadir of Roman glory.

The Goths returned to their assault on the Empire. Shapur, the Persian monarch, once more determined to throw the Romans out of Syria. The plague raged. In these circumstances, Valerian led his army into Cappadocia against the Goths, but could do very little, because of the ravages of the plague among his troops. News reaching him of Shapur's invasion, he took his army into Syria and at first was successful. But at Edessa, the tide turned. Shapur met him with such an overwhelming force that it was useless to fight him. Valerian and his soldiers shut themselves up in their encampment, while Shapur waited outside: the plague was doing his work for him.

Soon Valerian's soldiers began to starve. They turned on him in anger, blaming him for their plight and demanding that he get them out of it. Valerian

172 Shapur I taking Valerian prisoner, cameo of the 4th century AD.

offered Shapur a huge sum of money to let his soldiers retreat in safety, the only course he could take, for his army could not fight. Money, however, was something the Persian did not need. He rejected the offer with contempt. He demanded to treat with Valerian in person.

Valerian, either showing great courage, or great foolishness, went to the meeting. Shapur immediately had him seized. The Persians then led off the Emperor of Rome, the successor to the great Caesars, bound, and a captive.

It is said that the triumphant Shapur heaped indignities upon him. He made him kneel by his horse, for use as a mounting block. The news of the capture shocked the whole world, except the one man who could have taken revenge. This was Valerian's own son, Gallienus. He ruled the Empire jointly with his father, and was perhaps not displeased to find himself ruling it alone. At any rate, he took no steps to save Valerian, who died in captivity. Shapur, according to some historians, flayed his dead body. He stuffed the skin with straw, carrying with him on his journeys this grim evidence of the collapse of Rome.

235

Odenathus

As seen from Palmyra, the situation was dark. On the one hand was the triumphant Shapur with the Roman Emperor his prisoner. On the other, was the Empire, beset with invaders from over the frontier, racked with plague and ruled by a new Emperor, whose rule was instantly challenged by usurpers. The attempts on the throne were no longer limited to the intrigues of one commander. There was a scramble for the Imperial purple. No less than nineteen men declared themselves Emperor at various times during the reign of Gallienus, who survived for ten years, until murdered by his own staff.

At this perilous time in her history, Palmyra found the man for the moment. Odenathus was a Senator of the city. Because of his great abilities he was regarded as the leading man of the place, and the Palmyrenes turned to him in their plight.

He was sagacious. The Roman Empire was tottering, Shapur triumphant. The Persian, with little effort, could have been king of all Syria, had he not contented himself with ruthlessly laying his conquests waste. He killed an untold number of people, filling ditches with the dead and leaving thousands to die of starvation. He then retired to his dominions. It was this man that Odenathus decided to court.

He sent Shapur a letter, and accompanied it with a present perfectly in keeping with his native city. It was a caravan of camels, loaded with costly goods. In the letter he sought the Persian's friendship. Shapur ordered all the presents to be cast into the Euphrates. 'Who is this Odenathus,' he demanded, 'who insolently writes to his overlord?' He invited Odenathus to come to his court but with his hands tied behind his back. If, then, he did not fall prostrate in front of the throne, Palmyra would be destroyed, and with it his whole race.

236

The reply of Odenathus would be incredible if it were not attested by more than one classical historian. The Palmyrenes were famous for their archers. They fought as auxiliaries in the Roman army, and had a formidable reputation. Odenathus declared himself King of Palmyra. He then proceeded to recruit an army from the towns and villages of Syria. He was readily followed, for his reputation in all the country stood very high, and his people were now determined to seek revenge against the Persian monarch.

With this scratched-together army he boldly attacked Shapur. His soldiers were gathered, in a large part, from the Bedouin of the desert. It was unlikely that such a band could succeed in a frontal encounter, when the Roman army failed. Instead, Odenathus surrounded the sprawling forces of the Persian, and harassed them. The Persian army was strong in bravery, but notoriously weak in discipline. Odenathus' forces were implicitly obedient to him, for he was a hero in their eyes. Thus, Semite met Persian – and the Semites won. Shapur's army, disorganized by the running fight, became a rabble. The haughty Shapur was forced to beat a disorderly retreat, leaving prisoners and a rich booty in Odenathus' hands.

Odenathus was now the uncrowned king of all Syria. It would not have been surprising if he had chosen to strike out for independence from the Romans. Equally, it would have been natural if his astounding success had raised suspicions in the mind of the Emperor Gallienus. This Palmyrene was by far the most outstanding man of the Empire at the time. He might reasonably do what all the world was doing, and aim for the throne. Perhaps he would have done had there been a legion to elect him. But he chose the wiser course, staying loyal to Rome.

This decision was largely due to the diplomacy of Gallienus. He is an enigmatic figure. The writer of his life in the *Augustan History* portrays him as capricious, idle, luxurious and effeminate. As province after province fell to the invaders, he coined (says the writer) feeble jokes about it, shrugging off the collapse of the Roman world as a thing of no importance. While barbarians ravaged and slew, he spent his time in such things as composing poetry, gardening and cooking, in all of which pastimes he is described as being very able.

On the other hand, he was capable of putting himself at the head of his army, going out to meet the invaders, and turning them back. One such occasion must suffice as an example.

The Goths had supplied themselves with ships in the Euxine Sea. With these they attacked the Bosphorus, fanning out into the Mediterranean. They sailed into the Piraeus: they attacked Athens itself. In AD 262 the city fell. The place which had been the fount of civilization, which had taught the Romans all they knew about art, architecture, poetry, music, and philosophy, was given over to a horde of unlettered Goths, bent on destruction.

They attacked the other towns of Greece with the same results, finally invading Epirus, just across the narrow Adriatic Sea from Italy itself.

At last, Gallienus moved. He led his army into Epirus. Instead of fighting the Goths, he negotiated with them. With extreme subtlety, he treated the Goths as though they were his cultural equal, going so far as to give Consular honours to their leader. The Goths, flattered, tired of their long rampage, and decimated by the fighting, withdrew, going back to the Euxine from where they had come.

Gallienus' tact showed itself again with Odenathus. He gave him the title of *dux* and later, the high honour of *imperator*. He showed no envy: he showed no fear of a rival, though nineteen others were disputing the purple.

Scholars have questioned the *Augustan History* for a long time, until now they put down the writers as forgers and liars. Were Gallienus' faults all invented? They may have been. On the other hand, he may have been a dilettante at everything but being an Emperor in a world that was crumbling about his ears. However that may be, the task of meeting so much trouble exhausted him. In the last years of his reign he did little to stem the flood of ruin. He died in a conspiracy led by one of his commanders.

Odenathus met the same fate. He was killed in a palace conspiracy, but that was not the end of the story of the spectacular rise of Palmyra, because he left his kingdom to his second wife, Zenobia, famous in both legend and history, and her son.

Zenobia

Vaballathus, the son, was a mere infant: Zenobia, on the other hand, was one of the most phenomenal women in the history of the ancient world. She was compared to Cleopatra: it was, indeed, a comparison that she often made herself. She was very beautiful, in the dark and sultry Syrian way. (She may have been Jewish: at least the Jewish historians claimed that she was.) Like Cleopatra, she combined a strong physical attraction with a keen intelligence. She made a scholar and a critic her principal advisor. He was Longinus, a man so famous in his time for the profundity of his mind that his name has been attached for centuries to the treatise on aesthetic appreciation called *On the Sublime*, which he did not write. Zenobia had long discussions with him, astonishing everybody with the brilliance of her intellect.

She was, however, no bluestocking. Nor was she content to remain at home, enjoying the luxuries and intrigues of palace life. She would go hunting with her husband, a dangerous business, for he was a passionate hunter of wild beasts. She often wore the arms and armour of a soldier, and would march miles on foot with them. Besides her native Aramaic, she spoke Latin, Greek and Egyptian. She, it is recorded, wrote a book of history.

We need not implicitly believe all these things – beautiful Queens are inclined to dazzle people who write about them – but there can be no doubt that she had exceptional gifts. Her husband had been a highly successful man, much honoured, as we have seen, by Gallienus. Perhaps the best evidence of Zenobia's character is that, when Odenathus died, Gallienus looked upon his wife with considerable suspicion. He refused to give her infant son his father's resounding titles. Claudius, the Emperor who briefly followed him, did the same. Zenobia replied to this pointed snub by crowning herself Queen of the East, a fairy-tale title which did no harm to her growing legend.

Observing the troubles in which the Empire was plunged – the pressing barbarians, the empty treasury, the discontent of the people – this remarkable woman decided it was time for Palmyra to have an empire of its own. She did not *rebel* against Rome: with considerable statesmanship, she simply ignored it. Rome itself was occupied with a new danger. The Germans were coming through the Alpine passes and invading Italy itself. Soon Zenobia had taken the key city of Antioch, where she minted her own coins. From there this new Cleopatra decided to take Egypt. She dispatched an army of 70,000 men, which soon succeeded in conquering the country. Palmyra now had an empire stretching from Cappadocia and Galatia to the Nile. It was ruled in name by a child, but in fact, by a woman.

It may have gone to Zenobia's head: she took an unwise step, the first in her brilliant career. She abandoned her caution and threw off Palmyra's allegiance to Rome, naming her son Augustus, an Imperial title. The coins she had struck hitherto had carefully included the Roman Emperor's head. This now disappeared and Zenobia's took its place.

Claudius had gone. After a reign of twenty-one months, he died of the plague. The son of an Illyrian peasant came to the purple. Aurelian was first and last a soldier, rising to his eminence through the successive ranks of the army. He was a man with a passion for discipline, managing to instil some into the disintegrating army. He was ruthless in his punishments to the extent of tying a soldier to two bent trees, which tore the hapless man apart when released. It is clear that such a man could not tolerate a rebellion.

But Zenobia could still hope that he would. Rome had never been in such peril since the times of Hannibal. Aurelian was forced to surround the city with a wall, built by the citizens because the soldiers were too busy stemming the barbarians. It did not seem likely that, in such circumstances, the Emperor would engage on another front.

Nevertheless, Aurelian took an army to Syria. Zenobia decided to make her stand in Antioch. Aurelian arrived there and encamped outside it.

175, 176 *Coins bearing the heads of Zenobia and of her son Vaballathus.*

Now Zenobia's crack forces, those which had brought her victory, were the cavalry. These wore complete armour of considerable weight. Aurelian, noting this, instructed his own cavalry to retire before them, luring them on to follow.

Zenobia's cavalry went into the attack outside the city. Aurelian's instructions were obeyed. Zenobia's men were led on a long chase in the hot sun which made them sweat profusely in their heavy armour. Soon they were exhausted. When Aurelian's men saw this, they turned on them and cut them to pieces.

It was a severe blow for Zenobia. To add to it, the inhabitants of Antioch were showing no enthusiasm for what might prove to be an unprofitable business. Other cities had opened their gates to Aurelian on his march to Antioch: even one which did not, Tyana, had been saved by Aurelian from being sacked when it surrendered. The ambitious woman in their midst was a danger.

Zenobia and her general decided it would be prudent to go. They would fight the war in and near their own city of Palmyra. But it was not a simple matter to leave Antioch. The citizens might well try to prevent the army from escaping, to show their loyalty to the Empire. A ruse had to be adopted. The Palmyrenes spread a rumour that the Romans had been defeated. A man was dressed up in the robes and armour of Aurelian, and it was claimed that he had been captured. The citizens were deceived, and Zenobia and her army left safely during the night.

Aurelian followed her into her own territories. Battle was joined at Emesa, eighty miles from Palmyra itself. Once again Aurelian set his own light horse against the heavy armed cavalry of Zenobia, but this time the Palmyrenes had learned their lesson. They cut Aurelian's mounted forces to pieces. Aurelian called the legions into play in the traditional manner. They defeated Zenobia's infantry, and put them to flight. They then turned their attention to the cavalry, who in the confusion of battle had left their rear open to attack. The slaughter among them was great. Zenobia and her general, Zabdas, shut themselves up in Palmyra. Fortifications were hastily constructed, Zenobia going to the length of tearing down some of Palmyra's great buildings for the sake of the stone.

Zenobia trusted to an even more powerful defence than walls. This was the desert that lay around Palmyra. Outside the green city, there were few oases, and food there was none. With this double defence, she waited confidently for help from the Persians. Aurelian was decidedly in trouble, with scanty supplies and a hostile population: to add a second stuffed Emperor to his first was a prospect which would no doubt have tempted Shapur. But at this juncture, Shapur died: the massive help that Zenobia expected never came.

Aurelian laid siege to Palmyra, but he had no easy conquest. The Palmyrenes fought stoutly, even gaining the propaganda victory of wounding the Roman Emperor with a lance. Aurelian's position was now so dubious that he tried to open negotiations with Zenobia. Showing great spirit, she refused. She was now, without doubt, a true heroine.

Heroism, however, was no match for a pragmatic soldier. Aurelian took the unheroic course of bribing Zenobia's allies in the desert to stop harassing his supply lines to Emesa. They agreed: Aurelian could now feed his troops. But Zenobia could not. The people in Palmyra began to grow hungry. A small column of Persian troops coming to their aid may have raised their hopes, but they were dashed when Aurelian captured it.

177 *The treasury at Petra.* ⟩
178 *Overleaf: a view of the theatre.*

Left without allies and with a starving army, Zenobia turned as pragmatic as Aurelian. She decided to run away. The Queen of the East mounted a dromedary and fled through the desert. It is a romantic vignette of history. It caused even the sober Edward Gibbon to lose his head. Describing it, he adds a footnote glowing with praise for dromedaries, which, he avers, could outrun any horse – a surprising statement, since, a line or two later, he records the fact that Aurelian's cavalry caught up with her sixty miles away from Palmyra, taking her prisoner.

Being courteous to beautiful royalty within one's power had been a tradition since Alexander the Great had been magnanimous with the wife and daughter of Darius. Aurelian treated the captive Zenobia with respect. Bringing her before his throne, he asked why she had rebelled. She is supposed to have replied, with both dignity and guile, that she did not consider Aurelian's two predecessors worthy of the name of Emperor of Rome; according to her only Aurelian deserved that title. It is a highly improbable remark, since, had she made it, the blunt soldier would certainly have replied, with justified irritation, that she had rebelled against *him*.

In cold fact, she behaved poorly. Aurelian had already punished some of the rebels with death. Faced with the same fate, Zenobia first blamed the whole thing on her advisers, then named them. After this abject surrender, she was told her life and that of her son would be spared so that they could decorate Aurelian's coming procession of triumph in Rome.

The sources give two versions of what happened. One story is that, crushed by shame at the thought of being dragged in chains through Rome, she emulated her model, Cleopatra, by committing suicide. Another is that she accepted the disgrace, walked in the procession, and subsequently did very well out of her docility.

The Triumph of Aurelian is such a famous page of history that it cannot be omitted. A Triumph certainly took place. Whether Zenobia was there or not we cannot be sure. It is not improbable. In view of her ready acquiescence in defeat, she might well have decided that a walk in the Roman sun was the better part of valour.

⟨179, 180 *Petra: exterior of an obelisk tomb, and an interior view.*

A Roman Triumph consisted in a long procession from the Arch of Titus at one end of the Forum, along the Sacred Way to the Arch of Septimius Severus, up a steep incline on the Capitol Hill (on which one can still walk) to the Temple of Jupiter Capitolinus. Here the victor made an offering from his spoils.

The Triumph of Aurelian showed considerable showmanship. It opened with a parade of wild animals, followed by 1600 gladiators. This, like the parade of a visiting circus, showed the Romans what entertainment was in store for them in the days following the Triumph. Thus having lulled the citizens' basic anxieties, Aurelian proceeded to display the wealth he had brought them. This consisted of such things as gold plate, statues, chests of money and other eye-taking treasure. It was carried on wooden palanquins, each borne by four men. Delegations from conquered territories followed, then lines of prisoners, each body being preceded by a man carrying a placard saying who they were. The public's fancy was greatly taken by ten Gothic women who had fought beside their men.

Then came Zenobia's chariot, followed by Zenobia herself. She was so loaded with jewels that she almost fainted with the weight: it was not lost on the spectators that these jewels were now the property of the state. A golden collar was round her neck, to which was attached a golden chain, held up by a slave. Similarly chained, her son walked beside her.

Since nothing could cap that spectacle except Aurelian himself, he followed in a chariot drawn by four stags. Behind him came detachments of troops and the Senate. The procession started in the early morning and did not complete its journey to the Capitol until around three in the afternoon.

It must have been exhausting for Zenobia. She was rewarded by being given a villa in the countryside round Rome, where she lived out her days in peace and contentment – if, of course, she was not already dead by her own hand somewhere in Syria.

The Sands

Whatever the fate of Zenobia, it did not quench the hopes of the Palmyrenes. Knowing this, Aurelian gave orders to the Commander-in-Chief of the East, Marcellinus, to keep watch over them; to see, in particular, that they did not get any help from the Persians. A Palmyrene called Apsaeus organized a revolt with a number of others, with considerable duplicity. The aim was to maintain Palmyra as an independent kingdom, but first Apsaeus offered to declare Marcellinus the Emperor of Rome. The Palmyrenes were not, however, legionaries. They were merchants with a defeated army. Marcellinus listened to the offer, then informed Aurelian. He, with forced marches, brought the legions to Palmyra with unexpected speed. The merchants were caught unprepared. Aurelian took the city with ease and this time gave it over to the sack. He did not destroy the city: he did not even ruin its trade. But Palmyra was never again to play a major role in history.

The great days were gone. The caravans continued to pace through the colonnades, the merchants to worship in the great temple. But no new buildings were raised, except one. It remains today a gaunt ruin. A flight of steps leads up to a row of columns of which four remain. In the centre is the central chamber of a shrine. It is called the Temple of the Signa, because the Roman soldiers may have kept their standards there. In front of it stretch the remains of a camp, mathematically ordered, as ever. It was the camp built at the orders of Diocletian. After that nothing of any consequence was built, save some walls, which were raised by Justinian. By then the Emperors had left Rome. They ruled the Empire now from Constantinople. It was nearer to Palmyra than the old capital: Constantinople still needed the caravans and that was the reason Justinian defended the town. Little of his walls emerge from the sand today.

The barbarians at last took Rome and ruled it. Its majestic palaces and amphitheatres began to moulder, its population to dwindle, but Palmyra went on, quietly, industriously, making money but not squandering it on architecture. The Arabs came out of the desert, captured the city, and moved on to vaster conquests. It survived an earthquake in the eleventh century, but the end was in sight. By the fourteenth century, the trade routes had changed. Seamen were taking over from camel-drivers. The Palmyrenes withered away till only a handful of impoverished peasants huddled in a village which they built inside the Temple of Bel. The sand crept in, eating away at the columns, burying the city a little deeper each year.

The decline of Leptis Magna came more quickly, for it was afflicted by those ills which we have seen crowding in upon the Roman Empire. Poverty, plague, insurrections and oppressions ruined the trade on which it thrived. Leptis, too, had its barbarians on the frontier. They were the tribes in the interior. I have told how the legions kept them at bay. But as the power of Rome decreased, so did the boldness of the tribesmen. Leptis was attacked repeatedly. At last came the Vandals, sweeping into Africa and founding a kingdom.

The new Rome, at Constantinople, sent an army which defeated them. Belisarius, the victorious general, put a wall round the harbour so that his communications with Constantinople should be safe, but the rest of the city was neglected. The sands began to take over. Here, too, came the Arabs, but Leptis by now was semi-abandoned. The sands came further in, the people left. Leptis lay desolate. Its ruins became a quarry. Its columns were carried off to Europe, two hundred of them to Windsor Park, in England, where they still are.

By a coincidence, it was Justinian who raised the last building we can see in Leptis. It is thought to be a Christian church. It is now no more than walls built of large blocks, and some arches. But it is built of re-used stones, a sign that, even then, there were ruins in Leptis Magna.

181 *Columns from Leptis Magna in Windsor Great Park.* ⟩

182 *The rock-cut tombs of Petra.*

Epilogue in Petra

There comes a time for any student of history when he grows tired of it. Gibbon said that it was a record of the crimes and follies of mankind. This is a sombre enough remark: but the truth is worse. Crimes can be interesting, follies can have their charm. But when history repeats the *same* crimes, when men repeat their foolishness again and again in an identical mould, then weariness sets in. When in that mood the place to go is Petra. It has a history which nobody can deplore because we do not really know what it is. The 'rose-red city, half as old as Time' (as it has been labelled), is also a striking, almost unworldly, sight. It is the sort of ruin which, I fancy, all of us secretly hoped would be discovered on the far side of the Moon.

Petra is not rose-red. A recent traveller, John Knowles, has accurately described it as being the colour of smoked salmon. It is not a city now, whatever it was in the past. All that is significant in what remains of it today are tombs, so it is best called a cemetery. It is not so very old: in fact it is younger than the ruins here in Rome where I walk my dog. Yet Petra astounds, like no other place on earth, except, perhaps, the great Temple at Karnak. Amid the vast columns of that Egyptian monument one gives up thinking, composing, analyzing; one gives up dates and history, and simply enjoys the thought that men could make such a thing. So, at least, while one is there. Away from it, there is plenty of history to read, and the magic fades in the usual turmoil of blood and silliness. With Petra, the wonder remains, because Petra is a mystery.

I shall recount what we know, and it is little enough. A tribe of that people whose fortunes we have been following, the Semites, emigrated from the desert and settled in a place near the Gulf of Akaba which was little more welcoming

255

183, 184 *Two views of the city of Petra.*

than the place which they, the Nabateans, had left. It was a great, bare basin surrounded by mountains. The only approach was through a narrow cleft, like those in the story-books which lead to such places as Shangri-La. Today, to get to it, you ride a horse through the same cleft, and it is wide enough only for your horse and that of your guide. Since archaeologists must say something about such a strange rocky womb of a place, they maintain, in the teeth of plain sense, that it was eminently defendable. It was not: an invader had only to block off this narrow entrance, post companies of guards around the perimeter of the basin, and the inhabitants were sure to be starved out. The troops of Trajan conquered it with ease.

The truth is that, until the Romans came, few monarchs wished to conquer it. Petra was too useful. It lay on those caravan routes which, we have seen, were the arteries of the ancient world. The Nabateans were a peaceable people, busying themselves with trade and growing their food. They grew rich but not overwhelmingly so, like Carthage or Palmyra. They produced no geniuses; they threw up no great historical figures. They would have been forgotten save for one freak in their nature.

The traveller rides through the narrow gully for nearly a mile, often in deep shadow during the brightest day. He comes out to a triple arch which is the entrance to the town. Beyond it lies a great heap of ruins, divided by a Roman road. Here is the town which was made after the Roman conquest. There is an amphitheatre, a forum, a market place, a gymnasium – all the familiar appurtenances of Roman civic life. For anyone who has seen Leptis or, indeed, any of a dozen other Roman towns round the Mediterranean, they are not worth the ride. One barely looks at them for more than a single fleeting moment. One is overwhelmed by what lies around one.

The road drives straight at the vast circle of cliffs. They are honeycombed with tombs, hundreds of them, some simple structures with a dark, oblong entrance, with little decoration on the façade – these are the early ones – and other which have façades as elaborate as the fronts of Christian churches. All the bustling, noisy life of the trader's city took place as though in an amphitheatre, watched by a silent audience of the dead.

These tombs have been carved directly into the rock face. If, from a distance, they look pinkish, closer to they seem to have been painted over by inebriated theatrical scene-painters, drawing great brushes dripping with colour across the carved pillars and lintels. There are bands of green, of vermilion, of primrose yellow, deep purple, cool grey, and blue. They are the natural striations of the rock itself, used with profound art, to make tombs which are both solemn and festive. Sandstorms and time have smoothed the brilliant surface, till the façades seem to wave and shimmer, as though they were being seen through clear water.

This is striking enough. But to me, coming from Rome, there was something else, so strange as to be unnerving. Three great tombs stand out from all the rest. They are classical in design, with columns, capitals, doorways and windows. In what has gone before, we have been moving much amid this architecture, noble as in Leptis, stiff as in Timgad, or rich as in the fashion of Palmyra. In the seventeenth century of the Christian era, Italian architects in Rome had taken this style and studied its rigid rules. Artists such as Maderno, Bernini and Borromini, once they had mastered the art of building as well as the Greeks and Romans, tossed aside the rules and brought a new exuberance into architecture. Their façades curved and waved: they darted cornices into the sky: bulging masses contrasted with shadowed cavities: shape echoed shape like contrapuntal music. The classic style took on a new life, a new flourish. It even cavorted.

The Nabateans of Petra had done the whole thing for themselves in the first centuries after Christ. Here is the Baroque of Rome with all its new rhythms and daring, in a hot, stony valley in the desert. The façades of these tombs could be built again in the streets of Rome and they would be taken for churches. Yet they were built when the Christians were still a persecuted Semitic sect. How this creative miracle came about, no one knows.

I would have liked my Malabar uncle to have seen Leptis, and Palmyra. It might have opened his eyes to what mere *box-wallahs* can do. But he never left his plantations to the day of his death.

A Short Reading List

W. BEAVE, *The Roman Stage*, London 1964

M. BIEBER, *The History of the Greek and Roman Theatre*, Princeton 1961

J. B. BURY, *The History of the Later Roman Empire*, London 1923

G. CAPUTO AND V. CAFFARELLI, *The Buried City : Excavations at Leptis Magna*, London 1966

J. CARCOPINO, *Daily Life in Ancient Rome*, London 1941

FRANZ CUMONT, *Oriental Religions in Roman Paganism*, New York 1911

DIO CASSIUS, *Roman History* (Loeb, 1927, Vol. IX)

EDWARD GIBBON, *The Decline and Fall of the Roman Empire* (sometimes superseded, especially regarding Gallienus and Zenobia)

STEPHANE GSELL, *Histoire ancienne de l'Afrique du Nord*, Paris 1913–1929

VICTOR W. VON HAGEN, *Les Voies Romaines*, Paris 1967

DONALD HARDEN, *The Phoenicians*, London 1964

P. K. HITTI, *History of Syria*, London 1951

CH.-ANDRÉ JULIEN ET CHRISTIAN COURTOIS, *Histoire de l'Afrique du Nord*, Paris 1951

F. LOT, *La Fin du Monde Antique*, Paris 1927

K. MICHALOWSKI, *Palmyra*, London 1970

SABATINO MOSCATI, *The World of the Phoenicians*, London 1968

SABATINO MOSCATI, *Ancient Semitic Civilizations*, New York 1957

UGO ENRICO PAOLI, *Vita Romana*, Florence 1940 (Eng. trans. 1963)

H. M. D. PARKER, *A History of the Roman World from AD 138–337* (The annotated edition by B. H. Warmington should be consulted, London 1958)

GILBERT PICARD, *Le Monde de Carthage*, Paris 1956

M. ROSTOVTZEFF, *Social and Economic History of the Roman Empire*, 2nd edn., London 1957

Scriptores Historiae Augustae (an unreliable source: the Loeb edition, 1921, with critical notes, should be consulted)

J. B. WARD PERKINS, *Severan Art and Architecture at Leptis Magna*, Journal of Roman Studies, XXXVIII, 1948

List and Sources of Illustrations

Title-page
Temple of Bel, Palmyra, Syria
Photo A. F. Kersting

1   A Canaanite
Polychrome faience tile
Medinet Habu, Thebes, Egypt
c. 1150 BC
Museum of Fine Arts, Boston

2   Shipping cedar wood
Alabaster relief
Palace of King Sargon II (721–705 BC),
Khorsabad, Iraq
Louvre, Paris
Photo Hirmer

3   Felling cedars of Lebanon
Limestone relief
Temple of Amun, Karnak, Egypt
1318–1301 BC
Staatliche Museen, Berlin

4   Cedars of Lebanon
Photo courtesy Lebanese Embassy

5   Cuneiform alphabetic clay tablet
Ras Shamra, Syria
14th century BC
After Diringer

6   Table: development of the alphabet
After Dunand

7   Cylindrical watchtower dedicated to
Tanit and Bel
Limestone model
Carthage, Tunisia
4th–3rd century BC
Courtesy the Trustees of the British
Museum, London

8   Sarcophagus of King Ahiram of Byblos
with 10th-century Phoenician
alphabetic inscription on side of lid
13th century BC
National Museum of Lebanon, Beirut

9   Phoenician alphabetic inscription on
King Ahiram's sarcophagus (see no. 8)
After Diringer

10 Punic monumental alphabetic lettering
Limestone slab
Carthage, Tunisia
4th–3rd century BC
Courtesy the Trustees of the British
Museum, London

11 Map: orbit of Phoenician trade and
exploration

12 *Murex trunculus* shell
Tomb 79, Salamis, Cyprus
Late 8th century BC
National Museum of Antiquities,
Nicosia, Cyprus

13 Jug
Citium, Cyprus
8th–7th century BC
Ashmolean Museum, Oxford
Photo Eileen Tweedy

14 Dolphin and *Murex* shell
Obverse of silver shekel
Tyre
c. 460 BC
Photo Hirmer

15 Owl
Reverse of silver shekel (no. 14)
Tyre
c. 460 BC
Photo Hirmer

16 Exotic animals and plants from Syria
Relief
Festival Hall of Thothmes III
(1504–1450 BC), Karnak, Egypt
Photo M. Girodias

17 Ramses III (1195–1164 BC) attacking
Syrian fortress
Limestone relief
Medinet Habu, Thebes, Egypt
Oriental Institute, Chicago

18 Tribute from Tyre
Detail of Balawat bronze gates
9th century BC
Courtesy the Trustees of the British
Museum, London

19 Warship
Silver double-shekel
Sidon
c. 450 BC
Photo Hirmer

20 Galley
Silver shekel
Aradus
c. 350–325 BC
British Museum, London
Photo Ray Gardner

21 Galley, sea-horse and *Murex* shell
Silver shekel of Adramelek
Byblos
c. 360–340 BC
British Museum, London
Photo Peter Clayton

22 Town of Dagibu, and (below) impaled
Syrians
Detail of Balawat bronze gates
9th century BC
Courtesy the Trustees of the British
Museum, London

23 Dome of the Rock, Jerusalem
Photo A. F. Kersting

24 Air view of Jerusalem

25 Punic stele
Carthage, Tunisia
c. 4th century BC
Photo Roger Wood

26 Theatre, Leptis Magna, Libya
Photo Roger Wood

27 Harbour, Leptis Magna
Photo Roger Wood

28 Assyrian skin-covered coracle
Limestone relief
Palace of Sennacherib, Nineveh, Iraq
8th century BC
Courtesy the Trustees of the British
Museum, London

29 Two types of Phoenician ship
Drawing of limestone relief
Palace of Sennacherib, Nineveh, Iraq
8th century BC
Courtesy the Trustees of the British
Museum, London

30 Phoenician warship
Fragment of limestone relief
Palace of Sennacherib, Nineveh, Iraq
8th century BC
Courtesy the Trustees of the British
Museum, London

31 Roman merchant vessel
Relief on Phoenician sarcophagus
Sidon
c. 3rd century AD
Beirut National Archaeological
Museum
Photo Roger Wood

32 Air view of Carthage, Tunisia
Photo Dr Gus van Beek

33 Punic necklace
Carthage
Bardo Museum, Tunis

34 Female *protome*
Terracotta
Carthage
6th century BC
Bardo Museum, Tunis

35 Mask
Terracotta
Group II, Carthage
6th century BC
Bardo Museum, Tunis

36 Negroid mask
Terracotta
Group I, Carthage
6th century BC
Bardo Museum, Tunis

37 Phoenician gold bracelet
Tharros, Sardinia
7th–6th century BC
Courtesy the Trustees of the British
Museum, London

38 Necklace
Tharros, Sardinia
6th century BC
Courtesy the Trustees of the British
Museum, London

39 Necklace
Tharros, Sardinia
6th century BC
Courtesy the Trustees of the British
Museum, London

40 Eastern Phoenician cult statue of Astarte
Alabaster
Tutugi (Galera), near Granada, Spain
7th–6th century BC
Museo Arqueológica Nacional, Madrid

41 Melqart
Stele of Bar-Hadad
Tyre
Photo Syrian Department of Antiquities
and Museums

42 Melqart on sea-horse, and dolphin
Obverse of shekel
Tyre
c. 380 BC
Courtesy the Trustees of the British
Museum, London

43 Owl
Reverse of shekel (no. 42)
Tyre
c. 380 BC
Courtesy the Trustees of the British
Museum, London

44 Sign of Tanit
Roman mosaic
Sabratha, Libya
Photo Roger Wood

45 Precinct of Tanit, Salammbo, Carthage
8th–4th century BC
Photo Bardo Museum, Tunis

46 Phoenician infant burial
Precinct of Tanit, Salammbo, Carthage
8th–4th century BC
Courtesy the Trustees of the British
Museum, London

47 Priest carrying child
Punic stele
Carthage
Bardo Museum, Tunis
Photo Roger Wood

48 Air view of Leptis Magna
Photo R. Schoder, S.J.

49 Market place, Leptis Magna
Photo Roger Wood

50 West apse, Severan basilica, Leptis
Magna
Photo R. Schoder, S.J.

51 The Hunt
Roman mosaic
Hippo Regius, Algeria
3rd century AD
Bône/Annaba Museum
Photo Roger Wood

52 Antelope loaded onto a ship
Mosaic
Imperial Villa of Piazza Armerina,
Sicily
3rd–4th century AD
Photo Sonia Halliday

53 Arch of Septimius Severus, Leptis
Magna
c. AD 200
Reconstruction courtesy S. D. T. Spittle
Photo Brompton Studio

54 Sacrificial ceremony
Relief from Arch of Septimius Severus,
Leptis Magna
Tripoli Museum
Photo Roger Wood

55 Triangular cornice from Arch of
Septimius Severus, Leptis Magna
Photo Josephine Powell

56 Septimius Severus, Commodus and
Geta
Relief from Arch of Septimius Severus,
Leptis Magna
Tripoli Museum
Photo Roger Wood

57 Arch of Trajan (AD 98–117), Leptis
Magna
Photo Josephine Powell

58 'Annobal' inscription, theatre, Leptis
Magna
Photo German Archaeological
Institute, Rome

59 Head of Iddibal Caphada Aemilius
Marble statue
Leptis Magna
c. AD 15
Tripoli Museum
Photo U.D.F. – La Photothèque

60 Sailing boat relief, market, Leptis Magna
Photo Josephine Powell

61 Cargo boat relief, market, Leptis Magna
Photo Josephine Powell

62 Counters with dolphin supports,
market, Leptis Magna
Photo Josephine Powell

63 Linear measure, market, Leptis Magna
Photo German Archaeological
Institute, Rome

64 Standard volume measures, market,
Leptis Magna
Photo Roger Wood

65 Theatre, Leptis Magna
Photo German Archaeological
Institute, Rome

66 Statue of Dioscuros
Theatre, Leptis Magna
Photo Josephine Powell

67 Mimes, musicians and dancers
Roman mosaic
Aventine, Rome
Vatican Museum

68 Comic and tragic masks
Roman mosaic
Aventine, Rome
Capitoline Museum, Rome
Photo Alinari

69 Hadrianic Baths, Leptis Magna
Photo Roger Wood

70 Part of west apse, Severan Basilica,
Leptis Magna
Photo R. Schoder, S.J.

71 Portico of the Pantheon, Rome
Photo Fototeca Unione

72 Severan Basilica, Leptis Magna
Photo Roger Wood

73 Column capitals in west apse, Severan
Basilica, Leptis Magna
Photo Roger Wood

74 Reliefs in Severan Basilica, Leptis
Magna
Photo German Archaeological
Institute, Rome

75 West apse of Severan Basilica, Leptis
Magna
Photo German Archaeological
Institute, Rome

76 Fallen columns, Severan Basilica,
Leptis Magna
Photo Roger Wood

77 Personifications of Senate and People
Relief
Palazzo della Cancelleria, Rome
1st century AD
Vatican Museum

78 Philosophical argument
Fragment of relief
4th century AD
Museo Nazionale delle Terme, Rome
Photo Bulloz

79 Christian pulpit, Severan Basilica,
Leptis Magna
Photo German Archaeological
Institute, Rome

80 Medusa arcade, New Forum, Leptis
Magna
Photo Roloff Beny

81 'Proscaenium' inscription, theatre,
Leptis Magna
Photo Roger Wood

82 Phallic symbol on a door lintel, Leptis
Magna
Photo Roger Wood

83 Lighthouse, Leptis Magna
Photo Roger Wood

84 Harbour, Leptis Magna
Photo R. A. Yorke

85 Mooring rings, harbour, Leptis Magna
Photo Roger Wood

86 Wild beast hunt
Mosaic
Djemila, Algeria
Late 4th or early 5th century AD
Djemila Museum
Photo Marcel Bovis

87 Colosseum, Rome
AD 72–80
Photo Edwin Smith

88 Leopard hunt
Detail of fresco
Frigidarium of the hunting baths, Leptis
Magna
Photo Roger Wood

89 Roman gladiator's helmet
Before AD 79
Naples Museum
Photo Soprintendenza alle Antichità
della Campania, Naples

90 Roman gladiator
Bronze statuette
Courtesy the Trustees of the British
Museum, London

91 Orpheus and the wild beasts
Roman mosaic
Leptis Magna
Photo Josephine Powell

92 Fight between an elephant and a bull
Roman mosaic
Aventine, Rome
Museo della Civiltà Romana, Rome
Photo Arthaud

93–95 Gladiators
Mosaics
Torre Nuova, Rome
4th century AD
Galleria Borghese, Rome
Photo Mansell-Anderson

96 Bust of Commodus as Hercules
Marble
c. AD 190
Palazzo dei Conservatori, Rome
Photo U.D.F. – La Photothèque

97 Head of Septimius Severus
(AD 193–211)
Marble
Temple of the Severi, Djemila, Algeria
Photo Roger Wood

98 Head of Marcus Aurelius
c. AD 175
Museo delle Terme, Rome
Photo German Archaeological
Institute, Rome

99 Chariot race
Roman terracotta relief
Courtesy the Trustees of the British
Museum, London

100 Didius Julianus (Mar-June AD 193)
Obverse of gold aureus
British Museum, London
Photo Ray Gardner

101 Praetorian Guards
Relief
Hadrianic period
Louvre, Paris
Photo Giraudon

102 Model of ancient Rome at the time of
Constantine I by I. Gismondi
Museo della Civiltà Romana, Rome
Photo Arthaud

103 Pertinax (Jan-Mar AD 193)
Obverse of bronze sestertius
British Museum, London
Photo Ray Gardner

104 Septimius Severus (AD 193–211)
Bronze statue
Kythrea, Cyprus
Photo Sonia Halliday

105, 106 Consecratio denarius (obverse and
reverse)
Issue by Septimius Severus for Pertinax
(AD 193)
British Museum, London
Photos Ray Gardner

107 Septimius Severus and Julia Domna
offering sacrifice
Marble relief
Arch near the Forum Boarium, Rome
AD 204
Photo Alinari

108 Geta (AD 211–12)
Obverse of bronze sestertius
British Museum, London
Photo Ray Gardner

109 Arch of Septimius Severus, Rome, detail
AD 203
Photo Fototeca Unione

110 Bust of Caracalla
Marble
c. AD 211
Antikenabteilungen, Staatliche Museen,
Berlin

111 Elagabalus (AD 218–22)
Obverse of gold aureus
British Museum, London
Photo Ray Gardner

112 Sacred stone of Emesa
Reverse of gold aureus of Elagabalus
(no. 111)
British Museum, London
Photo Ray Gardner

113 Consecratio sestertius
Issue by Marcus Aurelius for Antoninus
Pius (AD 138–161)
British Museum, London
Photo Ray Gardner

114 Apotheosis of Antoninus Pius and
Faustina
Relief
2nd century AD
Vatican Museum

115 Mithraic rites
Roman wall-painting
Palazzo Barberini, Rome
Photo Fototeca Unione

116 Isiac ritual
Wall-painting
Pompeii
Before AD 79
Museo Nazionale, Naples
Photo Mansell-Brogi

117 Bust of Julia Mamaea (?) (d. AD 235)
Marble
3rd century AD
Palazzo Capitolino, Rome

118 Bust of Alexander Severus
(AD 222–35)
Marble
First half of 3rd century AD
Louvre, Paris
Photo Maurice Chuzeville

119 Bust of Maximinus (AD 235–38)
Marble
3rd century AD
Louvre, Paris
Photo Maurice Chuzeville

120 Payment of taxes
Stele from Kostolac
2nd century AD
Narodni Muzej, Belgrade
Photo Antonello Perissinotto

121 Burning of tax records in AD 118
Relief
Forum
Photo Fototeca Unione

122 Air view of Timgad, Algeria
Photo Compagnie Aérienne Française

123 Street intersection, Timgad
Photo Josephine Powell

124 Air view of Timgad
Photo Fototeca Unione

125 Capitol, Timgad
Photo R. Schoder, S.J.

126 'Arch of Trajan', Timgad, detail
Photo Josephine Powell

127 View towards 'Arch of Trajan', Timgad
Photo Fototeca Unione

128 African estate
Roman mosaic
Oudna, Tunisia
2nd century AD
Bardo Museum, Tunis

129 Blessing the standard
Trajan's Column, Rome
Photo German Archaeological
Institute, Rome

130 Temple of the Spirit of the Colony,
Timgad
Photo Roger Wood

131 Street crossing, Timgad
Photo R. Schoder, S.J.

132 Theatre and town, Timgad
Photo Roger Wood

133 Triumphal arch, Timgad
Photo Roger Wood

134 Legionary and praetorian models
Museo della Civiltà Romana, Rome
Photo Alinari

135, 136 Figures of slaves in pillory
Bronze
1st century BC/AD
Courtesy the Trustees of the British
Museum, London

137 Square with sunken pool, Hadrianic
baths, Leptis Magna
Photo German Archaeological
Institute, Rome

138 *Frigidarium* of the Hadrianic baths, Leptis
Magna
AD 126–7
Reconstruction by Cecil C. Briggs
Photo American Academy, Rome

139 Men's baths, Timgad
Mosaic sign
Timgad Museum
Photo Roger Wood

140 Women's baths, Timgad
Mosaic sign
Timgad Museum
Photo Roger Wood

141 *Tepidarium* of the baths at Timgad

142 Air view of the baths of Caracalla
(AD 211–17), Rome
Photo Fototeca Unione

143 Athletes and their trainer
Mosaic
Baths of Caracalla, Rome
Lateran Museum, Rome
Photo Alinari

144 Antinous
Hadrianic baths, Leptis Magna
Tripoli Museum
Photo Josephine Powell

145 Wild beast entrance, theatre, Palmyra
Photo R. Schoder, S.J.

146 Temple of Bel, Palmyra
Photo A. F. Kersting

147 Forum, Palmyra
Photo A. F. Kersting

148 Colonnaded street, Palmyra
Photo Roloff Beny

149 Tower tombs
Valley of the Tombs, Palmyra
Photo Institut Français d'Archéologie,
Beirut

150 Soldiers
Fragment of a relief
Palmyra
2nd century AD
Louvre, Paris
Photo Maurice Chuzeville

151 Married couple
Limestone funerary relief
Palmyra
c. AD 130–50
Ny Carlsberg Glyptotek, Copenhagen

152 Funerary bust of Ammiat
Palmyra
2nd–4th century AD
Louvre, Paris
Photo Maurice Chuzeville

153 Painted exedra
Tomb of the Three Brothers, Palmyra
Photo Institut Français d'Archéologie,
Beirut

154 Air view of Palmyra
Photo courtesy the late Professor
A. H. M. Jones

155 Plan of Palmyra
Drawn by Ian Mackenzie-Kerr

156 Triumphal arch, Palmyra

157 Column and capital, Palmyra
Photo Roloff Beny

158 Column ledge, Palmyra
Photo Roloff Beny

159 Street of columns, Palmyra
Photo A. F. Kersting

160 Temple of Bel, Palmyra
Photo A. F. Kersting

161 Temple of Bel, Palmyra, interior
Photo A. F. Kersting

162 Temple of Bel, Palmyra
Photo Roloff Beny

163 Arab procession with veiled women
(right)
Relief on stone beam
Temple of Bel, Palmyra
c. AD 32
Photo M. A. R. Colledge

164 Bel (centre), Agli-bol and Jarhibol
Relief
Temple of Bel, Palmyra
c. AD 50
Louvre, Paris

165 Camel driver
Limestone funerary bust
Palmyra
c. AD 140–60
Ny Carlsberg Glyptotek, Copenhagen

166 Ottoman castle, Palmyra
Photo A. F. Kersting

167 'Beauty of Palmyra'
Limestone funerary bust
Early 3rd century AD
Ny Carlsberg Glyptotek, Copenhagen

168–170 Philip I, the Arabian (AD 244–49)
Reverses of *antoniniani* with hippo, gazelle
and lion, commemorating the secular
games
British Museum, London
Photos Ray Gardner

171 Bust of Philip I, the Arabian
(AD 244–49)
Marble
Porcigliano, Italy
Vatican Museum

172 Shapur I's victory over Valerian
Cameo
4th century AD
Bibliothèque Nationale, Paris

173 Bust of Gallienus
Marble
c. AD 260
Staatliche Museen, Berlin

174 Aurelian (AD 270–75)
Obverse of gold aureus
British Museum, London
Photo Ray Gardner

175 Zenobia (AD 267–72)
Obverse of tetradrachm
Alexandria mint
British Museum, London
Photo Ray Gardner

176 Vaballathus
Reverse of *antoninianus* of Aurelian
(AD 270–75)
Antioch mint
British Museum, London
Photo Ray Gardner

177 Treasury of 'El Khazneh', Petra
Photo A. F. Kersting

178 Theatre, Petra
Photo A. F. Kersting

179 Exterior of an obelisk tomb, Petra
Photo R. Schoder, S.J.

180 Interior of tomb, Petra
Photo Roger Wood

181 Columns from Leptis Magna
Windsor Great Park (Virginia Water,
Surrey)
Photo A. F. Kersting

182 Rock-cut tombs, Petra
Photo Roloff Beny

183 View of Petra
Photo A. F. Kersting

184 Petra from the Wadi Musa
Photo A. F. Kersting

Index

Figures in italic refer to illustration pages

ADONIS 56
Aegean islands 18, 25
– Sea 22
Aemilianus, Emperor 234
Aga Khan (Prince Karim) 51
Agli-bol (moon god) 220, *221*
Ajaccio, Corsica 64
Alexander the Great 45, 152, 249
Alexander Severus, Emperor 163, 164–8, *165*, 172, 206
Alexandria 147, 152; massacre 152–3; Temple of Serapis 149, 152
alphabet 14–21, *18*, *19*, *20–21*
Alypius 109
Antinoöpolis 199
Antinous *198*, 199
Antioch 147, 228, 241, 243
Antoninus Pius, Emperor *158*, 172
Aphrodite 56
Apollo 199
Aprittus 234
Apsaeus 251
Aquilae 227
Arabia 13, 22
Arabs 12, 13, 30, 206, 207, 229, 251; conquer Palmyra 217; destroy Tyre 40
Aradus 32, *34*
Aramaic language 202, 205
Arameans 13, 202, 206
Ararat 13
Artaxerxes 166
Assyria and Assyrians 13, 32, *34*, 40, *48*
Astarte (Tanit) 56, 57, *58*, 59, 60, *60*, 220
Athens, 238; Agora 91; Parthenon 67, 217
Attila the Hun 10
Augustan History 237, 238
Augustine, saint 109
Augustus Caesar, Emperor 23, 110
Aurelian, Emperor 241, *242*, 243–4, 249–50, 251
Aurelius Zoticus 161–2

BAAL (god) 201
Baalat (god) 56
Baal Hammon (god) 60
Babel, tower of 12

Babylonians 12
Balbinus, Emperor, 227, 228
baths, 59, *87*, 120, 191–7, *192*, *193*, *194*, *195*, 199
Bedouin 207, 213, 237
Bel (god) 220, *221*, 252
Belisarius 252
Bernini, Gian Lorenzo 213, 258
Bible 36, 46, 61; *Ezekiel* 31; *Judges* 18; I *Kings* 14
Bologna 97
Borromini 258
Bosphorus 147, 238
'bread and circuses' 105, 109
Brindisi 104
Britain 104, 135, 147, 187
Brittany 22, 47
brothels, *see* prostitution
Byblos 20, 31, 32, *34*, 56
Byzantium 68, 222

CALEDONIANS 143, 146
Caligula, Emperor 150
Camoglie, Italy 45
Canaanites 13, 14, 17, 18, 22, 23, 25, 29; *see also* Phoenicians
Cannae 65
Cappadocia 234, 241
Caracalla (Aurelius Antoninus), Emperor 143, 145–7, 149–53, *151*, 155, 156, 192, 201
caravans 202, 221, 222, *222*, 225, 227, 229, 236, 251
Carthage and Carthaginians 20, 22, 41, *50*, 51–53, *52*, *53*, 56, 59, 62, 64, 65, 109, 220; *see also* Phoenicians
catacombs 208
Cato 121
chariot racing 109, 121, *121*, 153
charity 129
Christianity 56, 97; worship 97–98, 99
Christians 120, 234; persecution of 234
Claudius, Emperor 240, 241
Cleander 124, 125
Cleopatra 40, 240, 249
Clodius Albinus 135, 143
coins, Roman 23, *126*, *132*, 140, *146*, *157*, *158*, *242*, *243*; value 129

Commodus, Emperor, son of Marcus Aurelius *116*, 117–25, 127, 129, 132, 133, 139, 140, 146, 172, 191
Commodus, Emperor, son of Septimius Severus 71, *73*
Constantine I, Emperor, 97, 130–1
Constantinople 225, 251, 252
Consuls, 120, 127, 140
crucifixion 113

DACHAU, Germany 10
Dacians 110
Damascus 217, 225
Danube 234
Darius 249
David, King of Judah 37
Decius, Emperor 234
Dio Cassius 120, 122, 123, 133, 140
Diocletian, Emperor 192, 251
Dioscuros 82, *83*
Djemila, Algeria *106*, *118*
dole, Roman 105, 107, 109

EDESSA, Mesopotamia 234
Egypt and Egyptians 17, 18, 22, 30, 32, 233, 241
El (god) 56
Elagabalus (Bassanius), Emperor 110, 156–63, *157*, 164, 201, 217
Elba 25
Emesa, Syria 155, 156, 157, *157*, 244
England and English 25, 46, 171, 181
Epirus 238
Etruscans 46
Euphrates 236
Evans, Sir Arthur 67
Ezekiel 31, 40

FAUSTINA *158*
frankincense 29

GADES (Cadiz) 53, 56
Galatia 241
Galilee 37
Gallienus, Emperor 235, 236, 237–8, *239*, 240
Gallus, Emperor 234
Gama, Vasco da 23
games, secular 232
Germans 166

Geta, Emperor 71, *72*, 143, 145, *146*, 147, 149, 152, 166
Gibbon, Edward 10, 229, 249, 255
gladiators and gladiatorial combat 109, *112*, *115*, 121, 123, 127, 250
gold 32, 37, 122, 140, 202, 250
Gordian I, Emperor 227
Gordian II, Emperor 227
Gordian (Caesar) 227, 228–9
Goths 234, 238, 250
Greece and Greeks 12, 30, 37, 238; alphabet 18; bathing habits 191–2; as sailors 46; statues 199

HADRIAN, Emperor 89, 160, 199, 201, 206, 226
Hannibal 65
Hanno 47
Haroun-al-Rashid 13
Hebrews 13, 14, 17, 31
Herculaneum 67
Hercules 120, 122, 123, 127
Hierocles 160, 162, 163
hieroglyphics 18
Himilco 47
Hiram, King of Tyre 37, 40
hunting *70, 106*, 109, *110*, *111*, *111*; *see also* wild beasts

Iliad 37
India 9, 22, 23, 25, 122, 170, 200, 202
Indo-China 64, 190
Isis *156*, *159*
Italy 22, 166, 208, 241
ivory 25, 32, 139

JARHIBOL (sun god) 220, *221*
Jerusalem 12, *38–39*, 202; Dome of the Rock *36*; Temple of Solomon 14, 37, 217
Jesus Christ 13, 56, 71, 206
jewels 25, *54*, *55*, 122, 170, 202, 225, 250
Jews 12, 14, 160, 187
Julia Domna 143, *144*, 147, *149*, 155
Julia Maesa 155, 162–3
Julia Mamaea 155, 162–3, *162*, *164*, 166, 168
Julianus, Didius, Emperor *126*, 127–36
Julius Caesar 90, 139, 182
Julius Solon 139
Justinian, Emperor 251, 252
Juvenal 67

KARNAK *16*, *32*, 255
Kerala, India, 22, 23
Khorsabad, Iraq *15*

Knossos 31, 67
Knowles, John 255
Koran 13
Kythrea, Cyprus 138

LAETUS 132
Lawrence, T. E. 13
Lebanon 17, 30, 32, 51; cedars of *15*, *16*, 17, *17*, *37*; Mount 32
Leptis Magna 65, 67–116, *101*, *111*, *114*, 117, 155, 169, 200, 207, 252, *253*, 258; Arch of Septimius Severus *71*, *72*, *73*, *74*, *75*; Arch of Trajan 75, *179*; Basilica *69*, *88*, 89–98, *92–94*, *95*, *99*; Chalcidium *66*; Christian church 252; Hadrianic Baths *87*, 191, 192, *192*, 197, *198*, 199; harbour *44*, 102–107, *103*, *104*, *105*; Market Place *66*, *69*, 75–6, *78–79*; New Forum *100*; Temple to Jupiter Dolichenus 102: theatre *42–43*, *66*, 76–77, *76*, *80–81*, *82*, *83*, *84*, *89*, *101*
Libyans 67
London 9, 53, 91, *179*, 189, 222
Longinus 240

MACAULAY, Rose 9, 10
Macedonians 40, 141
Macrinus, Emperor 153, 155, 157
Maderno, Carlo 258
Marcellinus 251
Marcus Aurelius Antoninus, Emperor 117–19, *119*, 120, 129, 146, 158, 172; *Meditations* 117–18, 120
Mark Antony 206
Martial 67, 94, 113
Martialis 153
Marx, Karl 13
Masada, Israel 187
Masinissa 75
Maximinus, Emperor 166, *167*, 168, 226, 227–8
Maximus, Emperor 227
Melqart (god) 56, *58*
Mercury 122
Mesopotamia 13
Milan 225
Minoans 30–31
Misenium 135
Mithras 156, *159*
Mohammed 13
Moloch 62
Murex trunculus 28, *29*

NABATEANS 257, 259
Naples 10, 59, 104

Napoleon 64
Naraz 166
Narcissus 127
Nash, John 91
Nebuchadnezzar 32
Nero, Emperor 113
Niger, Gaius Pescennius 134, 135, 142, 143
Nile 199, 241
Noah 12
Noricum 141
Numidia 227

ODENATHUS 236–8, 240
oil: olive 37, 104, 105, 109: petroleum 67
On the Sublime 240
Orpheus 113, *114*
Ostia 81, 222
Oudna, Tunisia *180*
owls *28*, *58*

PALMYRA (Tadmor) 202–32, *203*, *205*, *208*, *211*, *212*, 226–7, 236–8, 241–4, 249, 251–2, 258; Agora 221, 222; Forum *204*; funerary temple 223; Great Colonnade 213, *214–15*, 217; Ottoman castle 223, *223*; portrait statues *224*, *225*; Temple of Bel *204*, *216*, 217–20, *218*, 252; Temple of the Signa 251; theatre 220; tower tombs *207*, *208*, *209*, *210*, *210*; triumphal arch *212*
Paris, Saint-Germain-des-Près 68
pepper 22–3, 29
Perennis 124
Persia and Persians 22, 40, 202, 206, 226, 228, 232–7, 244
Pertinax, Emperor 129, 132, *132*, *133*, 134, 136, 137, 139–40, *140*
Petra 255–9, *256*, *257*; theatre *246–7*; tombs *248*, *254*, 255, 258; treasury *245*
Philip the Arabian (Philippus, Julius Verus) 229, *230*, *231*, 232, 234
Phoenicians 13, 29, 30–32, 36, 197, 202; seamanship 45–47, *48–49*; trade and settlement *26–27*, 30, 51–55; *see also* Canaanites, Carthaginians and Leptis Magna
plague 228, 233, 234, 241, 252
Plautianus 145
Plautus 84
Plutarch 121
Pompeii 67, 91, 102
Pompey 90
postal service 200
prisoners of war 187, 250

Praetorian Guard 125, *128*, 129, 132–3, 135–6, 137, 145, 153, 157, 163, 164, 184, *188*, 228, 229; donations to 129, 132, 133, 134, 150; foundation of 129; pay and conditions 129, 141; recruitment 141

prostitution 161; brothels 120, 121, 191; religious 14, 59

Punic Wars 64–65

'purple' *see Murex trunculus*

Pylades 133

RAMSES III *33*

Ravenna 135, 225

rhetoric 94, 96–97, *97*

Rhine 166

Roman Senate and Senators 96, 122, 123, 129, 133, 134, 135, 137, 147, 152, 164, 226, 229, 250; choice of Emperor 127, 129, 136, 227, 228; declaring gods 119; decrease in power 141–2, 155

Romans 12, 23, 40, 46, *49*, 62, 65, 67, 147, 182, 206, 227

Rome 10, 29, 56, 64–65, 67, 68, 89, 104, 105, 130–1, 139, 147, 166, 222, 228, 232, 233, 250, 251–2, 259; Arch of Septimius Severus *148*, 250; Arch of Titus 250; Baths of Caracalla 150, 192, *195*, *196*; Campus Martius 90, 140, 232; Capitol 227, 250; Capitoline Museum 120; Castel Sant'Angelo 160; Circus Maximus 109; citizenship of 141, 201; Colosseum 68, *108*, 109, 110, 127, 160, 192; Forum 82, 110, 139, 149, 160, *171*, 250; Forum Boarium *144*; legal procedure 92, 94, 96–7; Monreale 225; Palatine 157; Pantheon 89–90, *90*; Quirinal 157; St Peter's 68, 213; Temple of Janus 229; Temple of Jupiter Capitolinus 227, 250; Testaccio 24; Torre Nuova *115*; Trajan's Column 110, 179, *183*

SABRATHA, Libya 58

sacrifices 59; animal 71; child 13, 61, *61*, 63, 135

Sallustia Orbinna 164

Salammbo, Tunisia 59, *60*, *61*

Sanskrit 23

Sardinia 22, 25, 53; Costa Smeralda 51

Sassanids 226–7

Scotland 190; *see also* Caledonians

seafaring 45–47, *78*

Sem (Shem) 12, 13

Semites 11, 12–13, *13*, 14, 30, 201, 237, 255; *see also* Canaanites, Hebrews

Septimius Severus, Emperor 65, 71, 73, 91, 92, 102, *118*, 120, 133, 134–6, 137–49, *138*, *144*, 145–7, 148, 149, 150, 152, 155, 160, 164, 166, 187, 190, 192, 200, 206, 226, 232

Shalmaneser III *34*, *35*

Shapur I 234–5, *235*, 236, 237, 244

Sidon and Sidonians 14, 18, 25, 29, 31, 32, 36, 49, 53, 56, 59, 62; shekel *34*

Sinai 18

slavery and slaves 13, 187, *189*, 197

Soaemias 155, 163

soldiering and soldiers 124, 147, 150, 155, 156, 157, 163, 166, 170, 172, 180–1, 182–90, *183*, *188*, *208*, 227, 233; *see also* Praetorian Guard

Solomon 14, 36, 37, 40, 206

Spain and Spanish 22, 25, 141, 184, 201

spices 170, 202

Stoics 91, 118

Suplicianus 133

Syria and Syrians 13, 18, *35*, 134, 147, 155, 160, 202, 225, 229, 234, 236–8, 241

TADMOR *see* Palmyra

Talmud 13

Tanit *see* Astarte

Taormina 81

Tavernier, Jean Baptiste 207

taxes 51, 107, 166, 169–72, *170*, *171*, 202, 233

Terence 84

textiles: linen 25, 32; silk 40, 202; wool 32

Tharros, Sardinia 53, 55, 59, 62; jewelry *54*, 55; shrine 55

theatre: masks 84, *85*, 86; mimes 84–85, 86; music 77, 84; productions 77, 84

Thrace 166

Tiber 24, 232

Tiberius, Emperor 71

Tiglathpileser I 32

timber 32, 37; *see also* Lebanon, cedars of

Timesitheus 228, 229

Timgad, Algeria 173–81, *174*, *175*, *176–9*, 182, 190, 207, 213, 258; Arch of Trajan 179–80, *178*, *179*, *185*, 186; baths 191, 194–5; Capitol 173; Temple of the Spirit of the Colony *185*; theatre 173, *186*

Titus, Emperor 110

tombs 55, 60, *207*, 208, *209*, 210, *210*, *248*, *254*, 255, 258

tophets 56–62

trade 18, 23, 25, *26–27*, 31, 46, 104

Trajan, Emperor 110, 172, 175, 179, 182, 201, 257

tribute 32, *34*, 36, 169

Tripoli 67

Tunis 59, *63*, 71

Tyre 14, 25, 29, 31–32, 36–37, 40, 51, 53, *58*, 62; shekel *28*, *34*, *58*

UNITED STATES of America 10, 64, 117, 222

VABALLATHUS 240, *243*, 249, 250

Valerian, Emperor 234–5, *235*

Valle, Pietro della 207

Vandals 68, 252

Vatican Council, Second 171

Vestal Virgins 56, 135, 162

Vetrivius Maerinus 136

Vietnam 10,

Vikings 22, 46

Vitellius, Emperor 129

Vitruvius 84

WARFARE, military *33*, 45; armour 184; *ballista* 187; bows 45, 184; javelins 45; phalanx 45, 184, 190; *pilum* 184; sieges 187; slings 45, 184, swords 45, 184; supplies 172 –, naval *34*, 45, 135

weights and measures 76, *79*

wheat 37, 104

wild beasts *32*, 104, 109–13, 203; bears 113, 122; elephants 65, 110, *115*, 135, 139; giraffes 110; jaguars 110; leopards 110, 111, *111*; lions 113; monkeys 32; ostriches 123; Polar bear 110; *see also* hunting – fights 111, *115*, 122 – shows 110, 113, 250

Windsor Park, England 68, 252, *253*

ZABDAS 244

Zenobia 238, 240–50, *243*, *249–50*